Alcohol :
Uses and Abuses

Margaret O. Hyde

ENSLOW PUBLISHERS, INC.

Bloy St. & Ramsey Ave.   P.O. Box 38
Box 777   Aldershot
Hillside, N.J. 07205   Hants GU12 6BP
U.S.A.   U.K.

Library of Congress Cataloging in Publication Data

Hyde, Margaret O. (Margaret Oldroyd)
  Alcohol : uses and abuses.

  Bibliography: p.
  Includes index.
  Summary: Describes alcohol and its effect on the body;
discusses the disease of alcoholism; and suggests ways
to resist peer pressure to use alcohol.
  1. Drinking of alcoholic beverages–United States–
Juvenile literature. 2. Alcoholism–United States–
Juvenile literature. 3. Drinking of alcoholic beverages.
4. Alcoholism. I. Title.
HV5066.H89   1988   362.2'92   87-12161
ISBN 0-89490-155-9

Printed in the United States of America

10 9 8 7 6 5 4 3 2

Illustration Credits

From *Getting in Touch with Al-Anon/Alateen,* copyright © 1980, by Al-Anon Family Group Headquarters, Inc. Reprinted with permission of Al-Anon Family Group Headquarters, Inc., p. 40; Nancy R. Goodrich, pp. 8, 11, 17, 23, 41, 48, 53, 71; Medical Center Hospital of Vermont, p. 31; National Institute on Alcohol Abuse and Alcoholism, U.S. Department of Health and Human Services, pp. 10, 41; National Institute on Drug Abuse, U. S. Department of Health and Human Services, p. 69; SADD Contract for Life used with permission, p. 80; SADD logo used with permission, p. 65; Courtesy of Joseph E. Seagram & Sons, Inc., p. 24; *World Health*, the magazine of the World Heath Organization, p. 15

Dedicated to Benjamin Williams Hyde

Contents

Foreword

Finding accurate literature for young readers has been exceedingly difficult in my twenty years as an alcohol educator. Myths and misconceptions abound in most of the books and pamphlets I've reviewed, and so, when asked what I would recommend as reading material for young people, I've had to reply, "Nothing."

Fortunately, the publication of *Alcohol: Uses and Abuses* has resolved my dilemma. Interesting, readable, and filled with facts, this book covers all the most important aspects of the use of alcohol.

Margaret Hyde has obviously researched the book with care. She covers everything from the chemistry of alcohol to the genetics of alcoholism in terms that can be easily understood—not an easy task with such a difficult topic.

Her greatest contribution is her factual discussion of the subject of alcoholism and its effect on the children of alcoholics. Practically no other book touches on these sensitive issues in such a non-blaming and helpful way. Because of her unbiased viewpoint, Ms. Hyde does not perpetuate the subtle stigma that keeps alcoholics and their families from seeking help. I'm sure this book will be of great help to children who have been lost in a morass of conflicting advice and ideas about alcoholism.

Not only will this book be of help to the children of alcoholics; it will also serve to educate those who keep misconceptions in place out of ignorance.

For the past twenty years, my life has been dedicated to teaching young people about the effects of alcohol and to reducing the stigma of alcoholism. It is a pleasure to finally have this excellent book as a resource.

Roberta Meyer

Member of the Board of Directors
of the National Council on
Alcoholism, Inc.

1

Alcohol:
The New Look

Alcohol has a new look on many fronts. From the introduction of beer with little or no alcohol to the increased acceptance of alcohol addiction as an illness, people are thinking about drinking in new ways.

Cindy's father is addicted to alcohol. He never feels comfortable without a certain amount of alcohol in his body, but he does not fit the picture that many people have of an alcoholic as a skid-row bum. Cindy's father is an executive who visits his favorite bar on the way home from work each night. When he reaches his house, he is argumentative, aggressive, and often abusive. Cindy is only five years old, but she knows how to dial 911 to call for help when her father beats her mother. She has learned that her father is sick, not wicked or weak-willed, but if you asked her opinion about alcohol, she would tell you it is bad.

Alcohol itself is neither good nor bad. It is the way that alcohol affects the behavior and health of those who drink it that is good or bad.

6

For most families, drinking alcoholic beverages is a pleasant experience. Kim and Brian are children whose parents drink socially. They drink wine with special meals, and sometimes they drink wine or other alcoholic beverages just to relax before dinner. They are like most adults who have between no drinks and three drinks a week. However, there is a new rule in this house that is part of the new look about alcohol. They refuse to serve drinks to anyone who shows signs of becoming drunk at their parties, and they arrange transportation for anyone who has managed to drink too much to drive. They know that court decisions in their state have held hosts who serve drinks to visibly drunk guests liable for damages.

Although drunkenness is not acceptable behavior in Kim and Brian's family, they will probably choose to drink when they are old enough to do so legally. They already feel comfortable about frowning on drunkenness and about saying no to alcohol and other drugs when peers put pressure on them to join the crowd. They are part of the new movement of young people who are saying no to drugs. While alcohol is an addictive drug for only about 10 percent of the population, it is an illegal drug for young people. Those who say no to drugs include alcohol among the drugs.

Recent laws are part of the new look about alcohol. Making drinking illegal before the age of twenty-one is largely a result of the growing awareness among people of all ages about one of the most serious problems in the United States. The leading single cause of death for the age group fifteen to twenty-four years of age is drunk driving. New campaigns to make highways safer from problem drinkers have grown in popularity with young people as well as older individuals and groups.

Many young people have joined the campaign for better fitness. Children as young as four are walking each day with their parents, young gymnasts have increased in numbers, and people of all ages are making great efforts to improve the conditions of their bodies. Many of these health-conscious people are saying no to alcohol as part of their training for a variety of events. The young people who join fitness programs feel comfortable saying no to friends who pressure them to drink.

Part of the new look is enjoying cocoa after skiing.

Part of the new look about alcohol is the trend toward drinking beverages with lower alcohol content. Many individuals who want to be part of the crowd drink nonalcoholic beer or light wine in an effort to cut down on calories or on alcohol consumption. The federal government permits drinks that contain as much as 0.5 percent alcohol to be labeled nonalcoholic. Although this is not much alcohol, there is no safe level for people who are at risk of becoming alcoholics. Problem drinkers who substitute these drinks tend to spend time with former friends in the same places as they did in their drinking days. This can make abstinence more difficult for them.

New information about alcohol itself has played a part in the new look. While social drinking is a pleasant part of the lives of most adults, one in ten of those who drink develop the disease known as alcoholism. Tentative tests are about ready at the present time to show which people will become alcoholics. There is new information that helps to warn those who are vulnerable to this disease because of genetic or other biological factors. Some experts still argue that environment plays a major role, while others say alcoholism may just be learned behavior. The facts that some people are alcoholics from their first drink and that there are alcoholics as young as seven years of age argue against this theory. Complex factors are involved, but evidence is pointing toward genetics and a major involvement of biological factors in the second most common disease in the United States. Certainly, individuals who never drink cannot become alcoholics, so abstinence is clearly a safe road for those who have alcoholism in their families. Although much remains to be learned, there is a new awareness of to alcoholism, now that it is more widely recognized as a disease. This is one of the most important parts of the new look.

Although there is a new look about alcohol that has developed because of new knowledge and new attitudes, almost everyone knows something about it. Cans and bottles of beer are often piled high at the front of a supermarket. Beer and wine are popular drinks at ball games, on camping trips, at parties, at picnics, and in many other places. Many people drink wine at dinner or have drinks before dinner. When someone asks for plain soda, a hostess or host knows that the request is for a drink without alcohol. Many cars have bumper stickers that show a symbol meaning, "Don't drink and drive." What people know about alcohol may make it seem good, or it may make it seem bad.

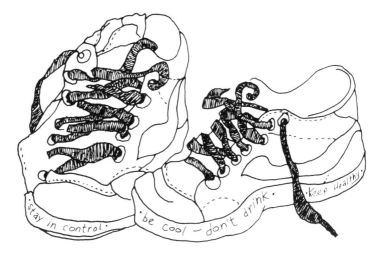

Many children grow up to drink much the same way their parents do. Very young children learn about alcohol without knowing it. They watch the adults in their families sip wine or beer with their meals. They watch them drink at other times. They listen to their families talking about alcoholic beverages, even in families where no one drinks. Many young people taste wine as part of religious services. Some older children join their parents in toasts at weddings and other celebrations.

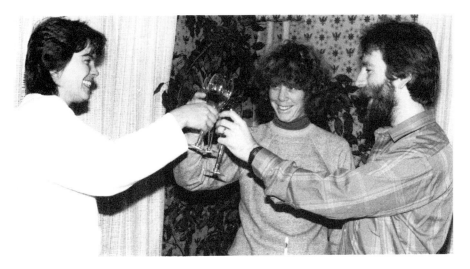

This family is celebrating a birthday with a toast. Their wine drinking is a pleasant experience.

You will have to decide at some time during your life whether you choose to drink. If you know the facts about alcohol, you can reach a more intelligent decision. If you choose not to drink, you can be more comfortable with that decision after you have examined the reasons why.

2

Alcohol: Yesterday and Today

Drinking alcoholic beverages is not new. People were probably drinking them long before they knew how to make any records of the kind we call history. Alcohol has long occurred in nature. Yeast, the kind used in baking bread, produces spores that are carried in the air, and these spores play a part in the natural process.

Picture some berries that are stored in a warm corner of a cave. Spores of yeast from the air fall on them and change the sugar in them to a crude wine. A cave man tastes it and feels the effects of the alcohol on his mood. This must have happened often long before people knew how to make beer or wine. Some wine is being made naturally today from overripe berries and other kinds of fruit. Perhaps you have watched birds and other animals feeding on overripe berries that may have some naturally made wine in them.

Beverage alcohol played a large part in the lives of many people who lived long ago. It was part of many worship ceremonies and was used in the practice of magic and medicine. Long before people learned how to make distilled spirits—such as vodka, gin, and bourbon—beer and wine were used to celebrate the making of war and of peace and to celebrate births, marriages, and initiations. Alcoholic beverages were drunk by friends as part of the traditional funeral ceremony, as a gesture of goodwill, and on many other occasions.

Then, as now, most individuals did not lose control of their drinking and found it a pleasant custom. No one knew about alcoholism in those days, but some individuals suffered from the disease and continued to drink until they were drunk. They drank so much alcohol that it led to social and personal trouble for them and those around them.

No one knows who was the first person to suffer from the disease called alcoholism, but there is a story about a person who may have been the first. It may or may not be true. Before the method of making wine was known, there was a Persian king named Jemsheed or Jamshid who was very fond of grapes. His servants stored grapes in jars so that he would have grapes to eat at any time of the year. One time, he discovered that the grapes in a jar were no longer sweet. The king had the jar labeled "poison."

A lady in the king's court who was suffering from severe headaches decided to drink from the poison bottle because she preferred to die rather than suffer the pain of her headaches. Actually, what she drank was crude wine, not poison, and she fell asleep. When she awoke, she felt better, so she sipped more of the "poison" from time to time. Although the wine helped her, it may have also given her a headache. She was forced to tell the king, who ordered that more of the "poison" liquid be produced. He and the members of his court enjoyed the new beverage, which, according to Persian historians, was the first wine.

Thousands of years ago, alcoholism was known only as drunkenness, and too much drinking was frowned upon then, much as it is today. Records of attempts to stop people from drinking until they became drunk were made long ago by Greeks, Romans, Egyptians, Japanese, Chinese, and others.

Gin Lane by William Hogarth depicts conditions in eighteenth-century England. The inscription over the door at the lower left side reads: "Drunk for a Penny, Dead drunk for Two Pence, Clean Straw for Nothing." Hogarth was against the drinking of distilled spirits, so this scene is probably an exaggeration.

One of the oldest temperance tracts was written in Egypt about three thousand years ago. It said:

> Take not upon thyself to drink a jug of beer. Thou speakest, and an unintelligible utterance issueth from thy mouth. If thou fallest down and thy limbs break, there is none to hold out a hand to thee. Thy companions in drink stand up and say: "Away with this sot." And thou art like a little child.

Beer drinkers in the Middle Ages.

In America, in 1619, just twelve years after alcoholic beverages were brought with the settlers of the Virginia Colony, a law was passed in an effort to control drunkenness. The first time a person was found drunk, he or

15

she was to be scolded privately by the minister. The second time, the scolding was public. The third time, the person was to be held on public view for twelve hours and to pay a fine. The custom of drinking was not unacceptable; drinking to excess was.

Laws did not stop alcohol problems in the Virginia Colony or in other times and places. About 1830, the trend was against distilled spirits, not wine and beer, with moderation as a goal. Gradually, people began to call for no drinking at all, and by 1919, it was illegal to make or sell any alcoholic beverage in the United States. Prohibition, as this time was called, was not successful in stopping those who really wanted to drink. Many people broke the law, and the law was repealed in 1933. Today, it is generally accepted that those adults who wish to drink have the right to do so.

Today, millions of people drink now and then to get a feeling of pleasure and relief from tension. It is such a familiar part of their life-style that many do not realize that alcohol is a drug. They stop after one or two drinks and have no desire to drink until they lose control. For them, drinking alcohol is a pleasant custom. However, one out of every three American adults say that alcohol abuse has brought trouble into their families either because of their own drinking habits or because of those of someone close. Today, estimates of the number of people who suffer from alcoholism reach about 12 million, an increase over estimates of recent years.

The increase in the amount of drinking is a growing concern for a number of reasons. Today, the number of high school students who get drunk at least once a month is more than twice as great as it was ten years ago. Recent reports show that many boys and girls are trying

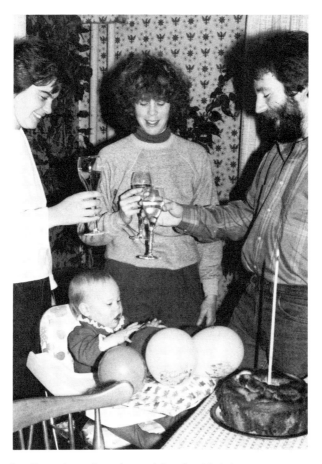

Many families enjoy wine when celebrating birthdays.

alcoholic beverages before they reach their teens and that some ten- to twelve-year-olds have alcohol abuse problems. Unfortunately, most of these boys and girls tried alcohol before they knew much about it.

Tom is a ten-year-old who used to empty the milk from his thermos and fill it with liquor before he left for school each morning. By the time he reached school, he was feeling the effects of the sips he took on the school bus. His teachers noticed that he was sleepy in class, but they did not think of alcohol as the cause of the problem.

After the bus driver reported Tom, the principal interviewed his parents. He discovered that his father was an alcoholic who drank so much that he never missed the liquor that Tom was using to fill his thermos. Tom's mother worked and left before the school bus arrived. Family therapy was suggested, and an appointment was made at the local mental health clinic for Tom and his parents.

Today, alcoholism is considered one of the most serious public health problems in the United States. About 65 out of every 100 people will be in alcohol-related highway crashes in their lifetimes. About four million drinking teenagers are showing signs that they may develop serious alcohol-related problems.

Scare tactics were used in the past—and sometimes are used today—in an attempt to frighten young people away from drinking. For many years, learning about alcohol meant learning all the bad things about it. A more meaningful approach is to help people drink sensibly, to learn the early signs of alcoholism, and to learn to feel comfortable about saying no to drinking.

Advertising of distilled liquor had already been banned from television when increasing numbers of people attempted to ban ads of wine and beer. Advertisers claimed that their aim was to get people to switch brands, not to get young people to drink or to get drinkers to increase the amount that they drink. However, images of drinkers as sophisticated and desirable linger long after the brand name is forgotten. There is continued controversy as to whether the ads promote excessive drinking, but they certainly do not show drunkenness, one of the possible undesirable and unattractive effects of too much drinking.

It is true that the media have helped to change the image of an alcoholic. Perhaps you have watched old movies in which the comic plays a drunk. In some old movies, a person who needs courage is shown taking a drink. These false roles have been discarded in most of today's entertainment. Today, the media seem more aware that there is nothing funny about suffering from an illness.

Through the years, people blamed alcoholics for being "weak-willed" or immoral. The stigma attached to alcoholism caused a great deal of harm. Today, most people recognize alcoholism for what it is: a tragic disease requiring treatment like any other illness.

Attitudes about drinking and driving have changed, too. Beverage alcohol affects the lives of everyone, even those who do not drink. The people who do not drink drive and ride on the same roads as those who drink too much to drive safely. Alcohol plays an especially prominent role in death and injury among young people. The average life span for most Americans is longer than it was in years gone by, but more children are dying at an early age. Alcoholism and accidents connected with alcohol abuse are blamed for this.

What you can do to help get the drunk off the road is described in a later chapter. If enough people will work together, our highways will be safer in the future.

Learning to drink responsibly and learning to feel comfortable about saying no to alcohol should begin before you need to make a decision about drinking. At this time, you can read about alcohol with less pressure from those who want you to drink or not to drink.

Alcohol
in Bottles

Alcoholic beverages in bottles and cans vary greatly in taste, use, cost, and the amount of alcohol they contain, but they all are produced by a process known as fermentation. In addition to the grapes mentioned in the last chapter, the sugars from other fruits can be changed to wine, too. Honey, sprouted seeds, grain, potatoes, and other kinds of fruits and vegetables can all be changed to alcoholic beverages in the presence of yeast and water.

Today, wine making is a delicate art. Most wine is made from grapes that are grown under special conditions to produce the qualities that are most wanted in wine. The alcoholic content of beverage wines—wines that are drunk with meals—varies from about 8 percent to 14 percent. Sherry, Madeira, and port are known as fortified wines and may have an alcoholic strength from 18 percent to 21 percent. In order to fortify wine, or increase the amount of alcohol in it, alcohol is added at the end of the fermentation process. Fortification is necessary because at a certain point in the process where yeast turns sugar into alcohol, the concentration of alcohol becomes too high for yeast to survive and fermentation stops. Expensive sparkling wines are made by adding extra sugar and yeast to start a second fermentation. Less expensive sparkling wines are prepared by cooling the wine and forcing carbon dioxide gas into it. Wine coolers are popular drinks in which wine and fruit juice are mixed together.

The fermentation process by which beer is made is known as brewing. Grain cereals such as wheat, barley, and rye are combined with yeast under the direction of a brew master. This person follows a special process often known only to him. Thousands of different varieties of beer are produced in countries in many parts of the world. They vary in ingredients, taste, and percentage of alcohol, but most contain between 3 and 6 percent alcohol. The light beers contain fewer calories, while the less popular LA (low-alcohol) beers contain about half the alcohol of regular brews. American beers are generally lager beers, which are bright, clear, and light-bodied beers. Heavier, dark beers like stout and porter have a slightly greater alcohol content.

Distilled spirits, or liquor, are made by distilling the soft, pulpy mass known as mash that results when the original ingredients are fermented to separate the alcohol and flavoring chemicals (congeners) from the residue and water. In this process, the fermented liquid is heated until it becomes a gas. Then the gas is collected and cooled, making it a liquid of more concentrated form. This makes the alcohol stronger. Gin, Scotch, vodka, whiskey, rum and bourbon are common distilled spirits. Their alcohol content is measured as "proof," with one degree of proof meaning 0.5 percent alcohol. Most of these beverages are 80 proof, or 40 percent alcohol. A beverage that is 90 proof is 45 percent alcohol, and one that is 100 proof equals 50 percent alcohol. People usually mix liquor, or distilled spirits, with tonic, water, soda, or fruit juice.

Whiskey marked 100 proof is not 100 percent alcohol.

Brandy, cognac, and cordials, often called liqueurs, are also distilled spirits. They contain between 20 and 65 percent alcohol and are usually quite sweet, so they are usually served in very small quantities and sipped slowly.

The taste of distilled spirits is not pleasing to the majority of young people when they are first introduced to them. This fact, along with the increased concern in America about health, about drinking and driving, and about getting ahead in one's career, has helped the popularity of many new kinds of alcoholic beverages such as wine coolers, liquor coolers, and low-alcohol (48 proof) cordials such as peach schnapps. Young people who enjoy the taste of chocolate and fruit juices have helped in the dramatic increase in the sale of new drinks with these flavors. In 1988, reports indicate decreases in the use of all illegal drugs among high school seniors with the exception of alcohol.

The trend toward moderation by the drinking of beverages with less alcoholic content appears to be a good one, but some individuals are concerned that drinkers will think they are as harmless as lemonade because they taste so much like fruit juice. The makers of the beverages claim that they make it clear that these lighter, sweeter drinks *are* alcoholic beverages and should be handled as such.

There is even controversy about the so-called non-alcoholic wines and beers mentioned earlier, which actually do contain a small amount of alcohol. Experts in the field of alcoholism don't think these beverages are a good answer for young people who want to belong to the partying crowd but who do not want to use alcohol. On the other hand, brewers note that bread and some natural fruit juices also contain small amounts of alcohol due to fermentation, and no one complains about this. They also claim that they do not market nonalcoholic beverages to people below the drinking age.

There are many kinds of nonalcoholic beer.

23

Many people believe that they can never develop a drinking problem as long as they stay away from the "hard stuff," meaning liquor. Marie's friends said she could not possibly be an alcoholic because she drank only wine. When she was hospitalized for health problems caused by drinking too much wine, it was discovered that she sipped wine all day long. Her erratic driving, which had bothered some of her friends, was easily explained after they learned that individuals can be just as addicted to wine as to other alcoholic beverages.

Knowing about alcohol means knowing the alcoholic content of different beverages, knowing how different amounts of alcohol affect the human body, and being aware that the same amount of alcohol can affect individuals differently.The alcohol in all alcoholic beverages is the same kind. The other ingredients may have some different effects on the digestive system, but the part that has an effect on the nervous system is the alcohol. Mixing drinks will not increase or decrease the effect.

All are equal in alcohol content.

12 oz.　5 oz.　1¼oz.

Alcohol may be familiar to many persons in a form other than beverage alcohol. Actually, there is a whole chemical family of alcohols. Some kinds are being used in fuel where there is a shortage of gasoline for automobiles. Certain kinds of stoves in boats use alcohol to heat food. Rubbing alcohol has been used for many, many years. It helps to stop the ache in tired muscles when it is rubbed on the body. Many boys and girls use this kind of alcohol on their faces when they are troubled with acne. Some people use it on their earlobes to prevent infection after they have been pierced for earrings. For young and old alike, rubbing alcohol is such a poisonous drink that it could kill a person who drinks it. In fact, some addicts have died from drinking it.

Beverage alcohol, called ethyl alcohol, is the most common kind. It is usually the one people mean when they talk about alcohol.

4

Alcohol in People

What happens when people drink alcohol as a beverage? This depends on many things, including the fact that each person is different, but the path which alcohol takes in the body is much the same for everyone.

Alcohol does not have to be digested, so it is absorbed quickly. About 20 percent of what is drunk is absorbed from the stomach and goes into the bloodstream. The rest of the alcohol goes into the small intestines and enters the bloodstream from there. Blood carries alcohol to all parts of the body, including the brain. Alcohol reaches the brain within minutes after it is drunk, and this is where the change in feelings takes place. At the same time, some alcohol which is passing through the liver is being changed from alcohol into water, carbon dioxide, and energy. The liver changes small amounts of alcohol each time the bloodstream carries its load through it. The part of the alcohol that is not changed continues to travel through the brain and other organs as the blood circulates through the body.

The liver works at a constant rate, so when there is more alcohol than the liver can change, it keeps on passing through all parts of the body, including the brain. The liver rids the body of the most toxic (poisonous) substances before it performs its normal duty of changing fats into energy. In other words, the fat from hamburgers, cheese, or butter that might have been eaten has to wait while the liver is working on the alcohol.

When too much fat accumulates in the liver, people develop "fatty liver," a condition that is reversible if drinking is stopped for a long enough period of time. However, spurts of heavy drinking can lead to a condition known as alcoholic hepatitis, and prolonged heavy drinking can lead to cirrhosis, a scarring of liver tissue and a disease that can kill. Individuals with hepatitis or cirrhosis must not drink alcoholic beverages at all.

Some drinkers are so addicted to the drug alcohol that they do not care whether their livers continue to function. Most people who drink alcohol for pleasure drink only small amounts that can be processed by the liver without much damage.

Most of the alcohol in the bloodstream is eliminated through the action of the liver, although sweating and breathing eliminate small amounts of it. However, heavy sweating and breathing do little to get rid of drunkenness. Exercise, hot coffee, or cold showers will not hasten the process. Give a drunk hot coffee and you have a wide-awake drunk. Walking a drunk gets you a tired drunk. A cold shower gets you a wet drunk. Although the amount of time it takes for alcohol to leave the body depends on individual differences such as weight and body chemistry, the fact is that it takes about an hour for the body to dispose of one ounce of liquor or one bottle of beer. It may even take two hours. There is no way to speed up the process except perhaps with a certain new, experimental drug that quickly reverses the effects of alcohol. This drug has been shown to block the intoxicating effects in rats, but scientists question whether it will suppress all the aspects of drunkenness. Since it does not lower the level of alcohol in the body, respiratory problems and coma that can result from excessive drinking may not be inhibited. If the drug is effective in humans, it may be limited to alcoholics. Such a drug will not be a quick fix for the headache known as the hangover.

Without any help from medicines of any kind, the effects of alcohol wear off in time through the action of the liver and through sweating and breathing. All the alcohol in the bloodstream is gradually eliminated. The liver is the only organ in the body that can use alcohol as a source of energy, and since it does not store the energy from alcohol as fat, some people believe that alcohol calories do not count. They do, however, because calories from alcohol will be used instead of those from food, and any leftover calories from food will be stored as fat. Calorie charts give different values for the amounts in various alcoholic beverages, but many show about 100 calories for a drink with distilled spirits (not counting those in the mixers) and slightly less for a four-ounce glass of dry (not sweet) table wine. Beer and ale are between 140 to 150 calories, and "lite" beer adds about 70 to 95 calories to a diet.

Alcohol does provide usable energy, but the calories are called empty calories because they contribute little or nothing to the nutritional needs of the body. Obviously, people who are dieting will do well to avoid alcoholic beverages. Not only do they add empty calories; they lower resistance to the snack foods that are usually served with drinks.

Mary drinks only a very small amount each evening before dinner. She has heard that this may help to prevent the buildup of cholesterol in her blood vessels and thus reduce her chances of heart attack. And there have been reports that a small amount of beverage alcohol will help the heart by relieving stress. With less stress, muscles will not squeeze as hard on the blood vessels, and the heart will not have to work so hard. Not everyone agrees with this idea.

Mary knows that alcohol in large doses can seriously damage her body, so she is very careful not to drink more than her usual small amount. New reports show a possible link between consumption of alcoholic beverages and the development of breast cancer in some women, but more remains to be learned. Mary has decided to continue her drinking pattern until there is further evidence, although she is considering exercise as a better way to relax.

Mary feels a warm glow almost with the first sip. This feeling has been helped by what she wants to experience and what she has learned from former experiences. Mary is not the only one who notices a change in mood after the first few sips of alcohol. If someone expects to feel relaxed or "high" when he or she drinks, this feeling may result even before alcohol reaches the brain. Experiments in which people have been told that they are drinking alcohol when they really were not have shown this to be true.

Why does a person's head ache after drinking heavily? Roberta Meyer, an alcohol and addiction educator, refers to such headaches, or hangovers, as "squished brain." When alcohol makes the blood vessels of the brain larger, the brain expands and pushes up against the skull. The blood vessels eventually go back to normal size and the headache goes away, but some of the cells are destroyed. There are billions and billions of brain cells, so losing a few is probably not serious. Some heavy drinkers do suffer from mental problems that may stem from the destruction of large numbers of brain cells, but authorities disagree about the importance of cell destruction in the case of moderate drinking. Ms. Meyer suggests heavy drinking is a little like playing Russian roulette. No one knows exactly which parts of the brain are going to be destroyed or what effect that damage will produce. Even though we don't use most of the cells, those that are destroyed just might be some that contain important information.

Awareness of the effect of alcohol on unborn babies has increased in recent years. Some babies whose mothers drank before they were born suffer from fetal alcohol syndrome, a pattern in which there may be mental, physical, and behavioral defects that are long-lasting. No one knows the full impact of maternal drinking in the lives of affected children. Nor does anyone know exactly what is a safe level of drinking for women who are pregnant. In most cases, fetal alcohol syndrome occurs in babies whose mothers have had considerable amounts of alcohol, but in some cases, the birth defects have shown up in babies whose mothers drank smaller amounts.

Researchers estimate that fetal alcohol syndrome occurs in about 1 to 3 per 1,000 births in the general population, but among problem drinkers, the rate has been shown to be as high as 23 to 29 per 1,000 births.

Much more remains to be learned about the effect of alcohol on the fetus, but it is certain that women who drink heavily during pregnancy run a greater risk of having smaller or deformed babies than those who drink rarely or moderately. Even though some authorities feel that the danger of small amounts of alcohol has been exaggerated, they recommend caution. In the absence of research establishing a safe drinking level during pregnancy, the U.S. surgeon general advises women to refrain from drinking during pregnancy or when considering pregnancy.

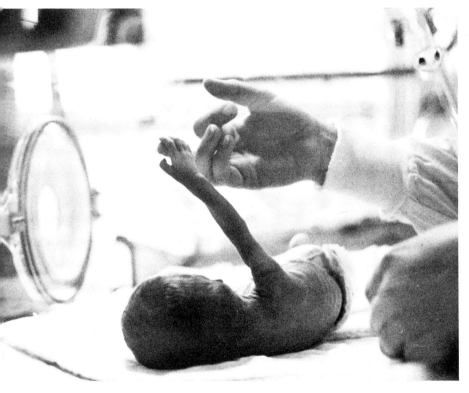

The infant above was born prematurely and was listed as a low-birth-weight baby. Research suggests that low birth weight is an effect of fetal alcohol syndrome. However, many other factors can also cause reduced birth weight.

Alcohol has been credited by many who drink with improving sexual relations. Certainly, it is true that small amounts of alcohol are a social lubricant that breaks down many inhibitions and increases the mood that initiates sex. This may be good in some cases, but in others, it is responsible for meaningless sexual relations that would not have occurred otherwise. Studies show a different kind of relationship between drinking and sex that is described best by a well-known quotation from Shakespeare's *Macbeth:* "it [alcohol] provokes and unprovokes; it provokes the desire, but it takes away the performance."

Long-term use of alcohol can lead to a condition in which the liver produces five times the amount of the liver enzyme that normally breaks down testosterone, the male sex hormone. Doctors have long noted that many male alcoholics develop feminine characteristics.

The immediate effects of alcohol on the human body and how long these effects last depend on at least three things: how much a person weighs, how much a person has drunk, and whether there is food in the stomach. If a person continues to drink frequently, the body builds up a tolerance to alcohol. This means that the individual needs more and more alcohol to get the desired "high." In some cases, physical dependence (alcoholism) develops, and the person feels sick without some alcohol in the body.

Sipping one drink, such as a twelve-ounce can of beer, has a mild tranquilizing effect on most people. Alcohol is actually a depressant, but it seems to act as a stimulant for some people when they first begin drinking. This happens because alcohol's first effects are on the part of the brain that controls behavior, such as self-control. With increasing amounts of alcohol in the bloodstream, vision becomes impaired, muscle coordination and balance are temporarily affected, memory decreases, and the mind has trouble getting things together. At this stage, one is considered drunk, which is a state of being physically and mentally handicapped.

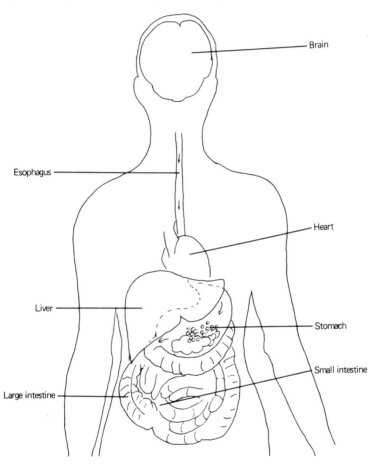

Alcohol reaches the brain more slowly when there is food in the stomach.

Fortunately, most people do not drink enough at any one time to have the above symptoms. Unfortunately, drunks may also suffer from drowsiness or aggressive feelings or severe depression. Very heavy drinking can depress the deepest levels of the brain, causing coma or death.

Most people drink just enough to increase awareness and pleasure. They drink to feel more relaxed and sociable. How much one drinks and how, when, and why all play an important part in whether drinking is an enjoyable experience or a sad one. If a person's mood is one of depression before drinking, alcohol may or may not increase that mood. No one knows beforehand how one will react to alcohol. Body rhythms, the time of day, attitudes toward drinking, drinking experience, and body chemistry are some of the things that play a part in individual reactions. So you can see that what happens when one person drinks the same amount of alcohol as another person may be quite different even when the kind of drink is the same. Suppose Jerry and Ken both drink the same amount of beer on the same day. Jerry is relaxing with friends and spends two hours drinking three cans of beer. Ken joins him after moving some heavy furniture. He is so thirsty that he gulps down his three cans of beer. You can easily see why Jerry and Ken have different effects from the same amount of beer.

How fast one drinks affects how much alcohol passes through the brain. Since the liver works at a steady rate, alcohol has a different effect on the brain when it is gulped than when it is sipped. Some people describe fast drinking as jolting the brain with sudden gushes of alcohol. The speed of drinking is just one of the things that make people react differently to the same amount of alcohol. In the above situation, the fact that Ken was tired added to the way his body reacted to the alcohol. He may have felt drunk, fallen asleep, been angry, started a fight, or acted in any of several different ways. Many of these reactions are well recognized by people of all ages as the state of being drunk even though they may have never tasted any alcohol.

Being drunk is being out of control of yourself. This is what most people want to avoid when they drink. This is what takes the pleasure out of drinking, and there are many ways to avoid this reaction unless you are prone to alcoholism.

5

Who Will Become an Alcoholic?

So far, there is no accurate test that can show whether a person will become an alcoholic, although the search is on for one that will show a risk of alcoholism. Doctors hope also to find a test that will show whether a person is drinking heavily. A new blood test for early liver damage may help doctors save many lives. Alcoholism is a killer, for it leads to traffic accidents, liver disease, certain kinds of cancer, and heart ailments.

As mentioned earlier, it is certainly true that most people who drink will never become alcoholics. They have no desire to increase the amount they drink, and they can give up drinking without any problem.

A person is probably not an alcoholic if for six months he or she can control drinking to no more than two drinks on any occasion and have no behavioral problems associated with drinking—such as driving while drunk, fighting with friends or parents, and inappropriate behavior. Unfortunately, many alcoholics manage to stop for a short time, but go back to their old habit after a few days, weeks, or months.

The answer to the question of what causes alcoholism is different for different people. Many studies of alcoholism have shown a much higher rate among family members of alcoholics than among people in general. Is alcoholism a learned behavior, or do hereditary factors play a role? Experts agree that alcoholism runs in families, but they disagree about why.

For many years, emphasis was placed on social factors, such as watching parents drink too much or living in a culture where drinking was frequent. Today, the emphasis is being placed on biological factors. Scientists are searching for genes that make people susceptible. Several kinds of alcoholism may exist. For some, getting into the habit of heavy drinking may be the main cause, while for others, heredity may be the most important factor. No one really knows. Many experts believe that both heredity and environment are involved.

Genes may even play a part in protecting against alcoholism in some individuals. For example, more women than men feel sleepy, sick, or dizzy after a drink or two. Many Chinese, Koreans, and other Orientals get red faces and have faster heartbeats and higher skin temperatures soon after they drink alcoholic beverages. Some experts think this protects them from excessive drinking. Japanese were once included in this group, but alcoholism is said to have reached epidemic proportions in Japan.

Experts who emphasize the biological role in alcoholism search for differences in brain function and small differences in the shape of the brain. New studies are being made to find out more about why the bodies of alcoholics handle the drug differently from those of non-alcoholics. For example, the sons of alcoholic men show the same kind of brain activity as their fathers do, according to a report by neurophysiologists Henri Begleiter and Bernice Porjesz and their colleagues at the State University of New York Health Science Center in New York City. Boys who never drank showed the same wave pattern even though they had never drunk alcoholic beverages. This suggests that the particular pattern of brain waves found in alcoholics, even those who stopped drinking, were not a result of their alcoholism.

Dr. Donald Goodwin of the University of Kansas Medical School studied children who were separated from their families at birth. These children came from both alcoholic and nonalcoholic parents. He found that sons of alcoholics were four times as likely to become alcoholics as sons of nonalcoholics even if they were raised by people who did not drink excessively. The sons of nonalcoholics did not become alcoholics at a rate any greater than the general population, even if they grew up in alcoholic foster or adoptive families. The evidence was not so clear for girls.

Other studies indicate a strong hereditary tendency, too. For example, one study in Finland and one in the United States showed that when one identical twin is an alcoholic, there is a greater than average chance that the other will be. But not every identical twin of an alcoholic suffers from the disease.

In 1986, Marc Shuckit, M.D., and his colleagues at the University of California at San Diego reported the finding that the response level of two hormones, prolactin and cortisol, differed in sons of alcoholic fathers from those in matched controls after they ingested alcohol. These researchers found that sons of alcoholics felt less drunk and showed less severe drunken effects, such as body sway, in the tests. Dr. Shuckit suggests that his findings and similar findings by other researchers may help physicians and the public to change their views of alcoholism since they show that biological and genetic factors may play a role.

Do these studies mean that you will become an alcoholic if you have an alcoholic parent? Not necessarily, but a person has a much greater tendency of becoming one than if this were not the case. Some may even have less chance of becoming alcoholics because they have an awareness of the problem and a warning that they have this tendency. Many experts suggest that anyone who has an alcoholic parent should not drink at all. Certainly, this is one way to be certain that they will not become alcoholics.

Alcoholism is not a matter of how much or how often one drinks. Some people need just one or two drinks to be out of control, while there are alcoholics who take many drinks and do not seem drunk. Alcoholism shows itself in different ways in different individuals, but dependency is a common factor.

People used to say it was impossible for young people to be alcoholics because they had not been drinking long enough for the condition to develop. Today, alcoholism is recognized as affecting people of all ages.

Many young people who want to stop drinking are finding help by joining Alcoholics Anonymous. They learn that they can still have good times while living sober. They meet people at the meetings who help them when they are tempted to drink again. In some places, young people in Alcoholics Anonymous have formed their own groups, although Alcoholics Anonymous is open to anyone who needs them. Its members include judges, rock stars, television actors, students, and retired people. They come from every race, religion (or no religion), and social class in the world today.

Help may come from a medical doctor, a teacher, a religious counselor, a school counselor, a hotline, or anyone trained to work with individuals who have alcohol problems.

You can get in touch with Al-Anon or Alateen by phone or by writing to them.

There are many self-tests and quizzes that have been prepared to help people learn whether they are developing alcoholism. Here is one that was prepared by the federal government.

1. Do you think and talk about drinking often?
2. Do you drink more now than you used to?
3. Do you sometimes gulp drinks?
4. Do you often take a drink to help you relax?
5. Do you drink when you are alone?
6. Do you sometimes forget what happened while you were drinking?

7. Do you keep a bottle hidden somewhere for quick pick-me-ups?
8. Do you need a drink to have fun?
9. Do you ever just start drinking without thinking about it?
10. Do you drink in the morning to relieve a hangover?

This test was designed for adults. Four or more yes answers mean an alcohol problem, but there are alcoholics in the early stages who may not even have four positive answers. One cannot diagnose alcoholism by a simple test such as the one above, although a test can help as a warning sign.

Alcoholism has been called a disease of denial. Anyone who is worried about whether he or she might already be an alcoholic should seek help. In addition to Alcoholics Anonymous and the people mentioned above, they may wish to consult the organizations listed at the end of this book.

Alcoholism can be treated.

41

6

Young Alcoholics

Are there really three million alcoholics under the age of eighteen? No one really knows the answer to this question, partly because there is no good definition of alcoholism.

Patty drinks to defy her parents. She cannot talk to them about her problems because they insist they know all the answers. Even though Patty admits they know more than she does about some things, she would like to tell her side of the story. Although they say they listen to her, she feels that they don't really hear what she is saying.

Patty's parents do pay attention to her in a way that upsets her. They keep watch over her to try to find out whether she has been drinking. When she comes home from a party, they smell her breath. They search her room looking for evidence that she might be hiding a bottle of beer there. Patty knows that her parents are especially anxious because her grandfather drank so much that he lost his job and caused a great deal of pain for his family in many ways. Patty tried to tell them that they are overreacting, but she was so discouraged that she almost decided to drink just to spite the parents who treat her like a prisoner.

One day, when Patty's parents were talking about the son of a friend who stole a car after he was drinking, Patty's father told her that he would beat her in public if she ever took a drink. Patty decided she would have a few drinks whenever she wanted. She really liked the feeling, so she continued to drink more often. Last Saturday, she passed out at a party in front of her friends, and she was really embarrassed when they woke her at the end of the evening to tell her to go home.

The morning after the party, Patty decided she could not face her friends without a drink. She felt much better after she drank some wine that she had hidden in her room. She sipped wine from time to time, and she began to feel that she needed it before she faced anything unpleasant. Before long, she began to wonder if she might be an alcoholic. She told herself that couldn't be true. She was only fifteen.

Another young alcoholic named Charles has a poignant story to tell. Charles's father was an alcoholic.

I'm Charles, seventeen, a high-school student and an alcoholic. I started drinking at the age of twelve. I was hanging around with an older group of kids and I drank to be "cool." Nothing much happened from my drinking until I was fourteen. By that time I looked older than I was, and I could buy beer or liquor without any trouble. The summer before I entered the eighth grade I started working in a gas station in a neighborhood where the people are very alcohol-oriented. My boss drank a lot, and he always had beer around the station. He encouraged me to drink. . . . I changed a great deal that summer and took a turn toward alcohol. I changed my attitude towards other people, got sloppy and careless, and started getting into fights.

By the time I started school that fall, I was drinking so much that I needed something every morning for some get-up-and-go. I started pitching in with other boys in the eighth grade to buy a case of beer so we could drink during school. We would hide it in some bushes near the school and go up there during recess. By lunch we would be pretty well totaled. The group of us started growing in number. The playground supervisor began wondering why half of the eighth grade were wandering up the hill during recess. Finally, he took a look—and found the beer. He let us off easy, just told us not to do it anymore. When we asked him what to do with the leftover beer, he said to put it in his car. . . . It was a fun year. I got drunk every weekend. . . . It seemed like everybody in the eighth-grade graduating class was drunk. One boy fell down as he was about to get his diploma.

I left home that summer, caddied for a country club, and lived in the clubhouse. At night, friends and I would go bar hopping. One night in a Washington bar, I got up to talk to a pretty girl who had smiled at me. The next thing I knew, I was coming to in an alley. . . .

I moved back with my father and entered junior high school. I started smoking pot, but it was making me lose the desire to do things. So I cut it out and started drinking booze again. . . . By the time I got to the tenth grade, I was keeping a six-pack of beer in my locker at all times. . . . I went out for the football team and would have been a starter if I hadn't been drinking. . . .

I turned into a superderelict. I didn't care about school or anything, just drinking. I started getting the D.T.'s. I stayed drunk all the way through the next summer. In the fall, I went out for football again. The coach kept me on the bench most of the time because he knew I was drunk. He put me in one game at the very end as a fullback. I couldn't get going, and about twenty guys piled on me. . . .

It took an accident to get me straightened out. I was driving alone and started to hallucinate and crashed into the median strip of a highway at about fifty miles an hour. I was knocked unconscious for about ten minutes. When I came to, I decided it was time to do something about my drinking. Since I already belonged to Alateen, I knew about Alcoholics Anonymous, and that's where I went for help. Now I haven't had a drink for six and a half months, and I'm staying sober one day at a time.

Rick tried a few beers when he was ten. He liked the way they made him feel, especially on days when he had tests. His parents drank so much beer that they never missed the cans he took from the refrigerator. During the next few years, every time Rick felt nervous, he managed to get hold of a few cans of beer. Sometimes he felt sick after he drank, but he decided that the only thing that fixed his hangovers was another beer.

Something strange happened to Rick one morning when he woke up. He couldn't remember what had happened the night before. Later in the day, he asked his friends about the evening, and they seemed surprised that he did not remember the plans they had made together to meet at the basketball court at two in the afternoon. Rick said he must have been drunk, but his friends insisted that he was fine. He had agreed with the plans and hadn't seemed at all drunk. Rick liked basketball. He was quite good. How could he forget making plans for the game?

What happened to Rick is not especially strange among people who are becoming alcoholics. In fact, it is a warning sign. Rick had a blackout. A blackout does not mean that a person becomes unconscious. Blackouts can happen to people who are not alcoholics as well as to those who are, but they are often an early warning sign of alcoholism. After a person has one blackout, he or she is apt to have more. Blackouts usually occur before the other early symptoms of alcohol addiction, such as heavy drinking binges and loss of control over drinking, in which people feel the need to sip drinks frequently throughout the day.

Even though not everyone agrees about the definition of alcoholism or about its causes, most experts agree that alcoholism can occur at any age. There are people who are alcoholics from the very first drink; they become totally out of control and continue to drink. Most people slide into trouble by gradually drinking more and more. Usually, there is no sharp line between the early stages of alcoholism and being just a heavy social drinker. Every disease has a beginning, and in many diseases, the first stages are mild and difficult to recognize. So it is with alcoholism. The earlier one knows what is happening, the better chance there is for recovery.

The physical effects of too much alcohol on young people are mainly nutritional. For example, when alcohol is acted upon by the liver, it uses up some of the B vitamins. Then they cannot be used for other important needs of the body. Alcohol also interferes with the use of some other vitamins.

Stay in control.

Many inexperienced drinkers do not enjoy the taste of liquor but continue to drink because of peer pressure. For some, this is the road to alcoholism.

When people drink heavily, they are not hungry for the kinds of food that their bodies need. Even though alcohol's calories are the same as those in candy, peanuts and other food, most alcoholics are thin because they do not eat properly. Both young and old alcoholics tend to suffer from lack of nutrients. Older alcoholics may suffer from serious physical problems such as liver disease, cancer, and brain damage.

Many young people who have alcohol problems will give up drinking altogether. Many will continue to drink but will become social drinkers—people who have no problem controlling the amount that they drink. Some, who are already alcoholics, will continue to drink heavily. They will go from stages of early alcoholism to late alcoholism.

society

7

Children of Alcoholics

Between 28 million and 34 million Americans have an alcoholic parent. In recent years, the long lasting effects of growing up in a family with an alcoholic parent have been getting much attention. Many adult children of alcoholics are affected by alcoholism many years after they have left their families. As children, their means of survival included three rules: don't feel, don't trust, don't talk about the alcoholic parent's problem. As adults, they share many traits, such as having difficulty with intimacy, suffering great anxiety with changes over which they have no control, guessing what normal behavior really is, and being extremely loyal even when the object of their feelings does not deserve it. They have a deep-seated conviction that no matter how well they do their jobs, their work will not be good enough to earn the approval and respect they so desperately need.

Many of these adults are joining support groups and attending workshops and conventions. More than 4,000 support groups of Adult Children of Alcoholics meet throughout the United States.

At least six million children are living with an alcoholic parent in the United States today. June is one of these children.

June could not remember when she first learned that her father was an alcoholic. Even before she knew what the word meant, she knew that her family was different from others. She knew that her father drank more than most fathers and that her mother was always nagging him about it. Alcohol played a big role in their family.

June wished she could find a way to make her family more like others. She wished her father would stop being very nice to her one day and mean to her many other days. Her mother told her he was mean when he had been drinking too much. She told June that she begged him not to drink, but it did no good. Telling him to stop drinking was not the answer. Even when she poured all his liquor down the sink, he managed to get some from a friend or at the local store.

Once in a while, June's father agreed to stop drinking forever, and June felt that he really tried. He would manage to keep his promise for several days or even a week, but then he began to drink again.

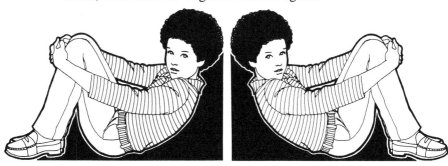

Children of alcoholics usually like their parents, but they do not like what they are doing.

Sometimes June found her father in the kitchen trying to sneak a drink without letting anyone know about it. She found empty beer bottles that had been hidden in strange places. June had learned at school that many alcoholics behave this way. She knew her father was suffering from a disease, but she did not know how to help.

June wondered if her father drank so much because she had not pleased him. She often came home late from a friend's house, and after he scolded her, he poured himself a drink. Perhaps she could make him stop by being very, very good. But June soon learned that this was not going to work.

June found a better way to cope with the situation at home when her class began to study the subject of alcohol abuse. Bill, one of the boys in her class, said he had been going to Alateen, a group for children of alcoholics, because his mother was an alcoholic. He said most people did not like to admit they were going because they did not want others to know there was a drinking problem in their families. He told the class that one could go without giving a name, but he didn't care who knew he attended the meetings. Everyone knew his mother was an alcoholic. Bill said he felt much better after he went to several meetings. It helped him understand his mother's behavior and helped him with his own life.

The meetings, where he could share his experiences with other young people who had similar problems, gave him comfort and support. He could talk about things there that he could not tell anyone else. Perhaps there was someone else in the class who would like to go with him.

June spoke to Bill after class, and he agreed to take her to a meeting. He promised not to tell anyone that she was going unless she decided she did not mind if others knew. June told her mother about the group. She thought her mother might like to go to the Al-Anon meetings, those open to all members of any family in which there was a person who had an alcohol problem. But June was wrong.

June was uncomfortable when she went to her first meeting of Alateen, but soon after she arrived, she found that everyone was very friendly. One of the first things she learned was that her father's drinking was not her fault. This made her feel much better. She also learned that there was not much she could do to stop her father, although she could suggest that he might feel better if he went for help at a group such as Alcoholics Anonymous. She learned that she was not the only one whose family had alcohol problems and that her father did not drink just to be mean.

June felt better when someone at a meeting said that he was embarrassed to bring friends home. June had often wanted to bring friends home on weekends, but she did not want them to see her father when he was drunk and angry. June tried to arrange to have friends after school before her father came home from work, but some days he came home early because he was drunk and needed to go to bed.

Mary, a close friend, said that everyone had problems with parents, and she acted as if seeing June's father drunk was not important. Susie, a new friend, said that her parents did not approve of drinking. She promised not to tell her mother, but June thought Susie might never come back. When Jane stopped by to see June one afternoon, she asked what was wrong with June's father. June told her he was drunk, but she wished she had a better answer.

At Alateen, June learned what to do when a friend was visiting at a time when her father had been drinking too much. She learned to ignore her father's behavior unless someone asked about him. Then she could say he was sick. This was certainly true, for alcoholism is a disease.

An alcoholic father loses control easily.

June looked forward to sharing more activities with her friends. She thought more about her own life and less about her father's alcohol problem. It was still there, but after June joined a community swimming program, she had less time to sit in her room worrying the way she had in the past. She even invited friends to her house and didn't worry about whether her father would come home.

One of the boys at a meeting of Alateen told about his life with two alcoholic parents. Sometimes he had to care for both his mother and his father, and the house was a shambles. Meals were casual, and there was seldom enough food in the house. The social worker who came to the meetings helped him to get a person called a homemaker to come in a few hours a day. Some of his aunts and uncles became more aware of the trouble, and they helped, too.

Many people at the Alateen meetings said that they felt their parents should make more effort to stop drinking. It helped them when they learned more about the addictive problem that is part of alcoholism.

No matter how hard June's father tried to stop, he was able to do so for only a week or two. During that time his body had to adjust to being without the chemicals in alcohol, and he probably felt very sick. When an alcoholic withdraws under the care of a doctor, medicine may be used to ease the unpleasant feelings. Sometimes it takes weeks, or even months, for the body to return to normal. With help, there can be recovery in both body and mind, and the person feels much better. Much depends on the amount a person was drinking and how long a period of time was involved.

If there is social pressure to drink, alcoholics can offer a variety of reasons why they are stopping for a while if they feel uncomfortable about saying they are alcoholics. "Doctor's orders" is a good answer to those who push them to drink. It is true that doctors order people who have drinking problems, or people who think they have drinking problems, to stop. People seem to accept this reason.

More and more people are learning about blackouts as a warning sign of early alcoholism. June learned at an Al-Anon meeting that many alcoholics suffer from blackouts. Mrs. Bryan told the group about her husband's problem of forgetting what had happened on the evening that she had asked him if they could go to the shore for the summer. He had pleasantly agreed that this would be fine, but the next morning he insisted that they had not discussed the subject. He denied ever saying that he agreed to going to the shore. Mrs. Bryan was upset for two reasons. She wanted to go to the shore and she felt that her husband had promised to take the family. She was also concerned that he could not remember something that was so important and that had happened so recently. She knew he drank a great deal, but she never connected this loss of memory with his drinking.

Even though June was not able to persuade her mother to go to Al-Anon meetings or to get her father to go to Alcoholics Anonymous, she felt much better since she had attended Al-Anon. She was able to tell her mother some of the things she learned there. Her mother no longer poured liquor down the sink or tried to hide it from her father. She no longer nagged her husband to stop drinking, something that had made him drink more.

June's family still was not a happy one. Although June had learned to be very self-reliant, she had always been afraid to trust other people. June and her mother learned to accept the fact that an alcoholic has to be the one to ask for change, and they hoped that June's father would do just that before things got worse. In the meantime, June could talk about her problems with people who understood and could help her cope with them.

8

What Would You Do?

Suppose you find yourself in any of the following situations at some future time. What would you decide to do? Sometimes there is no right or wrong answer, but some answers are better than others.

You have been babysitting for some neighbors. When they return from their party, you can tell that the man is drunk. He says he will drive you home after he gets a cup of coffee. You know that the cup of coffee will not make him sober. What would you do?

WOULD YOU DECIDE TO:

1. Ask to use the phone and call your parents to take you home;

2. If the mother is sober, ask her to drive you home;

3. Call a friend or relative and ask to be driven or walked home;

4. Try not to hurt the man's feelings, even if you have to drive with him;

5. Arrange beforehand to stay overnight if you have reason to believe you might run into a problem, or offer to sleep on the sofa if you have not made previous arrangements.

DISCUSSION:

You should not allow your judgment to be influenced because you might hurt someone's feelings. In this case it might be a question of safety for you and for others on the highway. If the man is drunk, he will not resent your objections after he has had a night's sleep. One babysitter remarked that her life was worth more than the money she got for sitting.

Your father is an alcoholic. This is creating serious problems for him and for the entire family. You want to help him.

WOULD YOU DECIDE TO:

1. Tell him that he would stop drinking if he loved you;
2. Learn all you can about alcoholism through an organization such as Alateen so you can help yourself;
3. Beg him to go to an Alcoholics Anonymous meeting;
4. Hide the liquor;
5. Ask your mother to go to Al-Anon;
6. Learn as many facts as possible about alcoholism.

DISCUSSION:

1. Your father probably does love you. His alcoholism is a disease for which he needs help. A family's attitude can help him.

2. If you are over twelve, Alateen meetings can be helpful. If you are younger or there is no group in your neighborhood, contact Al-Anon Family Group Headquarters. Some alcoholics resent their family contacting such an organization. You may need the help of a counselor at school, a religious organization, a community center, or someone you can trust to talk with.
3. *Begging* a parent to go for help seldom works.
4. An alcoholic will find some other sources when supplies are hidden. This may cause increased hostility.
5. If your mother is interested in finding help, Al-Anon may be an answer.
6. Contact the National Clearinghouse for Alcohol Information with a request for booklets for young people.

Your friend Mary has helped herself to a few beers from the refrigerator. She suggests you both ride your bicycles to the store for some potato chips. What would you do?

WOULD YOU DECIDE TO:
1. Go to the store alone;
2. Let Mary go to the store alone;
3. Find something else to eat;
4. Tell Mary you have to go home.

DISCUSSION:
If possible, persuade Mary to find something else to eat. If necessary, go home.

Your older sister is drinking secretly, and she wants you to join her. You know that she is troubled, but you

UNDER AGE ?

Don't ask us to sell you beer!

THINK TWICE...ABOUT DRINKING

cannot persuade her to ask for help. Last night, she told you about a wild drive with some of her friends who had been drinking. What would you do?

WOULD YOU DECIDE TO:

1. Continue to talk to your sister about her problems;
2. Drink with her so she will not pester you anymore;
3. Talk to someone your sister respects but who is not part of the family;
4. If you think your parents will understand, talk to them;
5. Tell your sister that her problem is so serious that either she must get help or you will have to talk to someone about it.

DISCUSSION:

While your decision depends somewhat on the individual situation, the fact that your sister is telling you about her problems may be a way of asking you to help. If you choose number 5, and carry through if she does not get help herself, you will be doing what must be done to prevent further trouble.

You are waiting for the school bus when the older brother of a friend drives up to you. He offers to drive you home. You would rather ride in his car than wait for the school bus, but you can tell that he has been drinking heavily by the way he acts and talks. What would you do?

WOULD YOU DECIDE TO:

1. Tell the drunken driver you plan to meet a friend on the bus;

2. Tell the driver you do not want to ride with him because he has been drinking;
3. Go with the driver and hope for the best;
4. Tell the driver you have other plans.

DISCUSSION:

If you tell the driver you have other plans, you will be telling the truth and can then avoid riding with a drunken driver. Trying to reason with a person who is drunk seldom accomplishes anything. Riding with a drunken driver is obviously dangerous.

You have reached the legal drinking age but have not had much experience with alcohol. You have just finished a can of beer. Someone wants you to mix drinks, but you think this might make you drunk.

WOULD YOU DECIDE TO:

1. Avoid mixing drinks;
2. At a later date, find out whether it is true that mixing drinks is dangerous;
3. Decide to limit the amount you drink.

DISCUSSION:

Limiting the amount of alcohol is more important than whether one mixes different kinds of beverages.

9

Choices

Whether one chooses to drink is a private decision. The number of very young people who are being pressured to drink by friends is increasing, but so is the number of young people who feel comfortable about saying no. At some point in growing up, you will have to decide whether you want to drink.

Fred had no problem deciding whether he wanted to join the beer set. He lives with an alcoholic mother. The tragedy of her life and the possibility that he may have a genetic trait that makes him vulnerable to alcoholism were both good reasons for his refusing to drink at all. When his friends ask him to join them in a few beers, he just says, "No, thank you," and he drinks a Coke, a non-alcoholic beer, or alcohol-free wine. He knows he cannot become an alcoholic if he does not drink.

Paul, on the other hand, comes from a family who disapprove of drinking for religious reasons. Paul drinks to rebel. Although many children in such families follow the behavior of their parents and avoid all alcoholic beverages, Paul started to drink at an early age. When his parents discovered this, he replied that they should be glad he was not using drugs. He did not realize that alcohol is a drug. Nor did he know that social drinking does not mean gulping down drinks, getting drunk, or feeling that drinking makes one macho. If Paul is lucky, he will be able to drink wisely when he reaches legal drinking age and will not get into serious trouble before then.

Sarah is the only one in her group who has not tried some beer or wine. One time when her friends called her chicken, she was ready with a good reply. Sarah told them that she would be chicken if she drank just to impress them. After that, no one paid much attention when she drank sodas while the rest of the crowd drank beer or wine.

Ben had a similar answer for the friends who taunted him when he refused to drink. He told them that if he drank to prove he was not chicken, he would just be showing them that he was afraid not to drink when they wanted him to. Ben's friends respected him for saying no to drinking alcoholic beverages.

Many young people are saying no for a variety of reasons rather than going along with the crowd. Emily decided not to drink because she is training for junior road races. She is careful about what she eats, runs three miles every day, and has very strong feelings about putting anything as toxic as alcohol into her body.

Molly does not drink for a different reason. She lives near the Terry family, who are very active in a group that is trying to get drunk drivers off the road. John Terry was only ten years old when he was killed by a drunk driver while cycling home from school. When the driver's case came to trial, he was given a very light sentence for his offense even though he had been arrested for drunk driving at an earlier date. The Terrys consider him a murderer, and they have lots of supporters.

Mrs. Terry has spent many hours working for the local chapter of MADD (Mothers Against Drunk Driving). She went door to door and talked to all the families in the neighborhood about MADD. A large number of neighbors, both young and old, joined her in raising funds, trying to change laws, and promoting the other causes of MADD.

Molly is collecting money to order a kit from SADD (Students Against Driving Drunk) that will help in starting a chapter of SADD in her school. Many of her friends are excited about joining the campaign to end tragic highway deaths and injuries even though they never knew John Terry. Some of them have already signed a SADD contract like the one on page 80 of this book.

The United Way reported recently that 39 percent of all high school seniors are problem drinkers. According to the National Council on Alcoholism, 6 percent are daily users of alcohol. It is obvious that laws are not stopping young people from getting and drinking alcoholic beverages. After the drinking age was raised in most states, many young people still managed to obtain alcohol.

Many problem drinkers wish they had never started to drink. Many just went along with the crowd. Role-playing helps individuals to be prepared with answers when they are approached by friends who want them to drink. Role-players assume the roles they are given and play them as they feel the person in that role would. Each player tries to think and feel just as the individual would when the situation happens. Role-playing has helped many young people to say no comfortably to friends who push them to drink.

Role-playing is a way to prepare people for many kinds of situations. For example, Secret Service men, FBI agents, detectives, and a variety of specialists who work with people are trained this way.

In a three- to five-minute skit with no plot, people can not only begin to understand how others feel about a situation but also practice making decisions about their own behavior without being defensive or overemotional before they have to make them in real-life situations.

Here is an example of role-playing in a class of eighth-graders.

John and Bruce are taking the roles of boys who want to get Karen to drink with them. They invite her to a party at the local parking lot on Saturday night, and they pretend to take along two six-packs of beer. At the parking lot, Karen refuses their offer of a beer, and they make fun of her. Karen says she just doesn't feel like drinking a beer. When they keep this up, she just walks away and joins another group.

"Don't you think you will be less popular with John and Bruce?" asks one of the boys in the discussion following the skit.

"Of course," Karen replies, "but there are other boys who have fun, too."

"Doing what?" asks another girl.

Karen reports about the disco that has started in her neighborhood where there is dancing and other entertainment, but no alcoholic beverages are allowed. The community provides some funding for it, and it has been a big success.

Some of the people in the class say that her answer is fine for her, but there is no such place where they live. Karen suggests they enlist the support of some adults and get one started or join a group such as STOPP or Just Say No Club whose activities are described below.

STOPP (Students to Offset Peer Pressure) began in Hudson, New Hampshire, in the spring of 1984 when a small group of students and a teacher, Mr. Peter Jean, began a program that is being copied in many other schools. The day Mr. Jean made an announcement over the school loudspeaker asking anyone interested in creating a drug and alcohol program to meet in his classroom after school, only about twenty-five students came. These people complained that there was not much for them to do in Hudson, where there was only one movie theater, and there was drinking and pot smoking at all the parties. How could they have fun without drugs?

What happened surprised a great many people. The first project of the group was to plan a dance where all drugs, including alcohol, would be prohibited. With the help of the Lions Club, which supplied the hall, and a local pizza parlor, which supplied cut-rate pizzas and soda, the first dance was a big success. About 175 people came. At the second dance, there were 250 people, and at the third dance there were 400. By the time the fifth dance was held, more than half the school attended.

The dances brought in enough money to pay for other activities, such as midnight cruises, mountain climbing, cookouts, and bowling. The program was even more far-reaching. STOPP grew into a network of groups that spread through many communities and involved people of different ages. STOPP is playing an important part in the trend toward making it acceptable not to drink alcohol or use other drugs.

All STOPP groups are independent from schools, but the groups are organized according to the grade level of young people. STOPP is the organization for high school students, and JUNIOR STOPP includes those in junior high. JUNIOR STOPP groups carry out programs that give young people a chance to enjoy recreation in a drug-free environment. They organize activities that will help relieve boredom and minimize idle time. They also provide factual information about alcohol and other drugs through youth-led programs. Older boys and girls who belong to STOPP help with JUNIOR STOPP programs.

The STOPP-A-TEER Club is an organization for younger children of a community (in preschool through grade 5). Through the clever use of puppetry, song, and dance, boys and girls are encouraged to avoid the use of tobacco, alcohol, and other drugs. Older boys and girls from STOPP and JUNIOR STOPP act as role models. They help to provide information and promote alternative activities to promote drug-free life-styles.

The motto of STOPP-A-TEER includes the statement that members are very special people who do not need alcohol or other drugs. Members take a pledge to say no to them.

Saying no to drugs is another large movement among young people. In January 1985, Tanisha Phillips, a fifth-grader in Oakland, California, suggested starting a club with the name Just Say No Club during the discussion of a film that her class had watched. Within a few days, there were as many as forty members of the club in her school. Several weeks later, Just Say No leaders spoke at a meeting of the National Ethnic Family Network. A month later, they were invited to the White House to meet Nancy Reagan, who gave her support to the program. As national chairman, she continued to encourage the formation of Just Say No Clubs far and wide.

The Just Say No Clubs are part of a tremendous movement of children aged seven to twelve that originated with inner-city blacks and Hispanics but has spread to hundreds of communities in the United States and to other countries. Children from many countries were invited to the World Kid's Congress in the summer of 1987 to explore solutions for stopping alcohol and other drug abuse and to start Just Say No Clubs all over the world.

Millions of members of Just Say No Clubs have joined to participate in parades, rallies, and other demonstrations. Each club has a captain who recruits other members and chairs meetings. The clubs provide continuing support for maintaining a drug-free life-style. They work with newspapers, radio, and television stations. Many media reporters are eager to find stories that show people who are involved in positive efforts of combating alcohol and other drug abuse. Important community members often lend their support by becoming honorary members of the clubs.

Like STOPP, Just Say No Clubs hold drug-free dances and sponsor other activities, such as block parties, picnics, sports events, and games. Local artists, printers, and advertising agencies are helping to publicize the groups and their cause. Millions of young people in all fifty states of the United States are participating in such programs. This new movement is making a difference. It may be the turning point for those who are afraid to say no to peer pressure.

An estimated 90 percent of the young people who get into serious trouble with alcohol and other drugs say they got involved because of peer pressure, according to some reports. Dr. Donald Ian Macdonald, administrator of the Alcohol, Drug Abuse, and Mental Health Administration, and special assistant to the White House for Drug Abuse Policy, has said that no other generation has had to cope with so much pressure at so young an age. He adds, "Those kids who do learn to handle peer pressure and think for themselves may well be the strongest, most responsible, finest youngsters that we have seen in this nation."

Many young people enjoy cider and encourage friends to do the same. This is a kind of positive peer pressure.

In November 1986, the National Federation of State High School Associations unveiled plans to help students cope with problems of alcohol and other drugs. With a budget of over $27 million for a five-year period, they launched the program in which student leaders visit schools to help make abuse out of style. Through a network named TARGET, these student leaders and athletes play an important part in trying to change the social norms.

You may wish to start a STOPP program, Just Say No Club, or similar club in your community or in your school. For those who think the programs will not work in their community, note that STOPP has worked in places like Belize in Central America, the third largest producer of marijuana in the world. Organizers of such programs say that if it will work in the jungles of Belize, it will work anywhere.

Throughout the United States the new trend of saying no to all illegal drugs (including alcohol, which is illegal for young people below the drinking age) is helping many young people to feel comfortable about resisting peer pressure. Just saying no is not the total answer to stopping the abuse of alcohol and other drugs. Much more remains to be done before boredom and peer pressure to use alcohol and other drugs are reduced in many communities. Many large social problems need better solutions. But you can make a difference by helping to provide alternatives to alcohol and other drug abuse and increasing the trend toward making it hip to say no.

* * * * *

Here are some suggestions offered by the National Institute on Alcohol Abuse to help young people feel comfortable about standing up to peer pressure when they are offered a drink:

No, thanks; if I drink I'll lose privileges.

No, thanks; I don't like the taste.

No, thanks; I've got to study for a test tomorrow and I need a clear head.

No, thanks; when I drink I usually end up embarrassing myself.

No, thanks; I have to drive home.

No, thanks; I'm on a diet. Liquor has a lot of calories. I'd rather eat.

No, thanks; I'm in training.

No, thanks; what else do you have?

No, thanks; I don't drink.

10

Is
This True?

1. Alcoholic beverages have empty calories; therefore, they do not count as calories in diet plans.
The first part of this statement is true, but the last is false. The calories in alcoholic beverages add weight to the body even though they have very little, if any, good nutritional value.

2. Most alcoholics are homeless people who do not want to work.
False. Only a small percentage of alcoholics fit the picture that most people have of alcoholics. The great majority of them live with their families and hold jobs. They include lawyers, teachers, nuns, doctors, factory workers, and just about all kinds of workers. Anyone, even a very young person, can be an alcoholic.

3. A problem drinker is the same as an alcoholic.
False. Many people who drink heavily never become alcoholics. Problem drinkers often become light or moderate drinkers without much effort. Alcoholics cannot do this.

4. People who become alcoholics have only themselves to blame.

False. Alcoholism is a physical disease. There are biological as well as environmental factors involved.

5. People who have alcoholic parents will become alcoholics.

False. Although there is a greater tendency for children of alcoholics to develop the same problem, knowing this can alert them to the problem and help them avoid becoming alcoholics. Certainly, not all children of alcoholics become alcoholics.

6. Alcoholism may be several diseases with a common outcome, much as cancer is many different diseases.

True. There may be at least two basic types of alcoholism, one with a genetic connection and one without. Some experts believe there are more than two types.

*7. Alcohol is the most commonly abused illegal drug among young people.

True. Alcohol is an illegal drug for more than 25 percent of Americans, those under the legal drinking age. Surveys indicate that it is much more commonly abused than marijuana, crack, or other illegal drugs.

8. A person who has been drinking heavily may carry on a conversation and not appear to be drunk while suffering from a blackout.

True. In an alcoholic blackout, information is not stored properly in the brain and may be completely forgotten the next morning. Even violent acts may be forgotten. In one study it was found that 28 percent of Eskimos who committed violent acts while drunk had no memory of what had happened.

9. Alcohol is a stimulant.
False. Although alcohol may have a stimulating effect for a brief period of time, it is really a depressant. Medically, alcohol is a drug that depresses the central nervous system, slowing the activity of the brain and spinal cord.

10. Problem drinkers and alcoholics are responsible for about two-thirds of the highway deaths involving alcohol.
True. Half of all fatal accidents involve drivers who have been drinking, and two-thirds of these are caused by people who have problems with alcohol.

11. A social drinker is more alert after a few drinks.
False. He or she only thinks this is true. Alcohol makes a person think that the senses are sharpened, but, in fact, they are not.

12. Alcohol affects different people differently.
True. It can even affect the same person differently on different occasions.

13. Black coffee, fresh air, and cold showers help people to sober up faster.
False. Alcohol is eliminated from the bloodstream by the liver over a period of time, and this time is not shortened by coffee, fresh air, or cold showers.

14. A can of beer is less intoxicating than the average drink of liquor.
False. A twelve-ounce can of beer, one ounce of 100-proof liquor (or one and a half ounces of 80-proof liquor), and a six-ounce glass of wine are equal in the effect on the body, but food in the stomach, fatigue, and other factors are involved in a person's reaction. Many

wine and beer drinkers still believe that they are consuming beverages that are less alcoholic than "hard liquor." The expression "only a beer" is misleading.

15. You can tell when a person has had too much to drink by the way he or she walks or talks.
False. Many persons who are impaired do not stagger when they walk or slur their speech when they talk.

16. Heavy drinking during pregnancy can have serious effects on the baby.
True. Women who drink heavily during pregnancy run a greater risk of having babies with smaller head size, lower birth weight, and mental retardation. It is believed that fetal alcohol syndrome is the third most common known cause of mental deficiency.

17. Alcohol is dangerous for snake bite, shock, and overexposure to cold.
True. Although the drinker feels relaxed and less concerned with minor irritations, the alcohol can have a negative effect on the body. In spite of the feeling of warmth, the body temperature is lowered after drinking alcoholic beverages, with the exception of cases where the body is overheated. Alcohol causes capillaries, blood vessels that carry blood just beneath the surface of the skin, to become temporarily large, so more blood travels through them. This causes a flushed skin and a warm feeling. The feeling is limited to the skin area, and the drinker is not really warmed since much internal heat is taken from his other organs to the skin. Actually, drinking in very cold weather can be dangerous.

18. One cannot overdose on alcohol the way one can with other drugs.

False. Large doses of alcohol can cause the heart to stop and the breathing center of the brain to cease functioning. Many young people who drink because of a dare or to show off have been taken to emergency rooms where their stomachs have been pumped in efforts to save them. Overdoses of alcohol account for more deaths in young people than heroin.

19. Alcoholism can be cured so that social drinking is possible.

False. Alcoholism can be treated, but alcoholics should not try to drink socially. This is a very dangerous myth.

Now you know something about alcohol. And you know enough to be aware that the effects of alcohol differ for different people. They even differ for the same person at different times.

Too much alcohol can have many different effects.
For example, it can . . .

make some people argumentative.

make some people silly and noisy.

make some people sleepy.

make it harder for some people to think clearly.

So far, no modern nation has been able to control the misuse of alcohol by prohibition laws, by taxing alcoholic beverages, by changing age restrictions on who may buy them, or by making rules about advertising them. Only people who know something about alcohol can make it a good thing or bad thing for themselves. Only people who know something about alcohol can know what is best for them.

CONTRACT FOR LIFE

A Contract for Life
Between Parent and Teenager
The SADD Drinking-Driver Contract

Teenager   I agree to call you for advice and/or transportation at any hour, from any place, if I am ever in a situation where I have been drinking or a friend or date who is driving me has been drinking.

_____
Signature

Parent   I agree to come and get you at any hour, any place, no questions asked and no argument at that time, or I will pay for a taxi to bring you home safely. I expect we would discuss this issue at a later time.

I agree to seek safe, sober transportation home if I am ever in a situation where I have had too much to drink or a friend who is driving me has had too much to drink.

_____
Signature

_____
Date

S.A.D.D. does not condone drinking by those below the legal drinking age. S.A.D.D. encourages all young people to obey the laws of their state, including laws relating to the legal drinking age.

Distributed by S.A.D.D., "Students Against Driving Drunk"

80

For Further Information

ALCOHOL HELPLINE
1-800-ALCOHOL
This national referral number can get you in touch with organizations
ranging from Al-Anon chapters to rehabilitation centers.

AL–ANON FAMILY GROUP HEADQUARTERS, INC.
P.O. Box 862
Midtown Station
New York, NY 10018

ALCOHOLICS ANONYMOUS
General Service Office
P.O. Box 459
Grand Central Station
New York, NY 10163

COAF (CHILDREN OF ALCOHOLICS FOUNDATION)
P.O. Box 4185
Grand Central Station
New York, NY 10163

MADD (MOTHERS AGAINST DRUNK DRIVING)
P.O. Box 1217
Hurst, TX 76053

NATIONAL CLEARINGHOUSE FOR ALCOHOL INFORMATION
P.O. Box 2345
Rockville, MD 20852

NATIONAL COUNCIL ON ALCOHOLISM
12 West 21st Street
New York, N.Y. 10010
1-800-NCA-CALL

NATIONAL HIGHWAY TRAFFIC SAFETY ADMINISTRATION
400 Seventh Street, S.W.
Washington, DC 20590

NATIONAL LICENSED BEVERAGE ASSOCIATION
309 N. Washington Street
Alexandria, VA 22314

RID (REMOVE INTOXICATED DRIVERS)
P.O. Box 520
Schenectady, NY 12301

SADD (STUDENTS AGAINST DRIVING DRUNK)
P.O. Box 800
Marlboro, MA 07152

Getting in Touch
With Al—Anon/Alateen

UNITED STATES

ALABAMA
Greater Birmingham Intergroup
P.O. Box 5514
Birmingham, AL 35255 • (205) 322-1500

Al-Anon Information Service
P.O. Box 565
Saraland, AL 36571-0565 • (205) 470-9160

ALASKA
Anchorage Al-Anon Intergroup
P.O. Box 200508
Anchorage, AK 99520 • (907) 276-6646

ARIZONA
Al-Anon Information Center of East Valley
55 East Main Street, Suite 109
Mesa, AZ 85201 • (602) 969-6144

Al-Anon Information Service
6829 N. 21st Avenue
Phoenix, AZ 85015 • (602) 249-1257

Al-Anon Information Service
5315 E. Broadway, Suite 106
Tucson, AZ 85711 • (602) 790-8922

Al-Anon Information Service Center
P.O. Box 4595
Yuma, AZ 85364 • (602) 783-2011

CALIFORNIA
Santa Clara Valley Al-Anon Intergroup
1 West Campbell Ave.
Campbell, CA 95008 • (408) 379-9375

Al-Anon Inland Empire Service Center
459 W. La Cadena Dr. Suite 2
Colton, CA 92324 • (714) 824-1516

Marin Al-Anon Intergroup
P.O. Box 400
Corta Madera, CA 94925 • (415) 924-3430

Oficina Intergrupal Hispana De Al-Anon
301 S. Harvard Blvd.
Los Angeles, CA 90020 • (213) 380-8139

Al-Anon Family Groups of Southern California
3431 W. 8th Street
Los Angeles, CA 90005 • (213) 387-3158

Modesto Information Service Office
P.O. Box 4324
Modesto, CA 95352 • (209) 524-2553

East Bay Al-Anon/Alateen Info. Services
477 15th Street
Oakland, CA 94612 • (415) 832-8258

Al-Anon Information Service
P.O. Box 3517
Pinedale, CA 93650 • (209) 442-4999

Al-Anon Tri-Valley Information Service
P.O. Box 1797
Pleasanton, CA 94566 • (415) 828-4611

District 13 Information Service
P.O. Box 614
Redwood City, CA 94064 • (415) 326-8672

Al-Anon Information Service
P.O. Box 60193
Sacramento, CA 95860 • (916) 446-4611

San Diego Al-Anon Family Groups Office
3108 Fifth Avenue Suite E
San Diego, CA 92103 • (619) 296-2666

San Francisco Al-Anon Information Service
50 Oak Street Room 505
San Francisco, CA 94102 • (415) 626-5633

Al-Anon Information Service of Orange County
2098 "F" S. Grand Avenue
Santa Ana, CA 92705 • (714) 545-1102

Al-Anon Intergroup of Santa Barbara
P.O. Box 30428
Santa Barbara, CA 93130 • (805) 962-1287

District/Intergroup Al-Anon
P.O. Box 2412
Santa Rosa, CA 95405 • (707) 528-3610

Delta Al-Anon Inf. Service of Stockton
8626 N. Lower Sacramento Rd.
Suite 18-7093
Stockton, CA 95210 • (209) 239-1162

Ventura County Al-Anon Intergroup
1325 E. Thousand Oaks Blvd.
Suite #102
Thousand Oaks, CA 91360 • (805) 499-7800

COLORADO
Pikes Peak Al-Anon Service Center
12 North Meade
Colorado Springs, CO 80909 • (303) 632-0063

Al-Anon Service Center
2801 E. Colfax, Room 204
Denver, CO 80206 • (303) 321-8788

Foothills Al-Anon Intergroup
P.O. Box 1207
Fort Collins, CO 80522

DELAWARE
Mary-Del Tri-Co. Al-Anon Information Service
P.O. Box 561
North East, MD 21901 • (301) 939-4690

82

DISTRICT OF COLUMBIA
Wash Metro. Area Al-Anon/Alateen
Information Service
c/o St. Paul's Episcopal Church
Rock Creek Church Road & Webster St.
Washington, D.C. 20011 • (202) 882-1334

FLORIDA
Palm Beach County So. Dist. 8C
Information Service
P.O. Box 928
Boynton Beach, FL 33435

Al-Anon Information Service
P.O. Box 14187
Bradenton, FL 34280 • (813) 722-3411

District 15 Al-Anon Inf. Serv. Liaison
P.O. Box 640
Cape Coral, FL 33910 • (813) 574-5882

Broward Al-Anon Information Service
P.O. Box 731
Fort Lauderdale, FL 33302
Telephone: (305) 537-1143

Al-Anon Information Service
P.O. Box 5313
Hudson, FL 33567 • (813) 847-0777

Al-Anon Information Service of Pinellas Co.
P.O. Box 1511
Largo, FL 33540 • (813) 446-5911

Dade and Monroe Al-Anon/Alateen
Information Service
P.O. Box 557264, Ludlam Station
Miami, FL 33155 • (305) 754-2583

Greater Jacksonville Al-Anon
Information Service
P.O. Box 2234
Orange Park, FL 32067-2234
Telephone: (904) 350-0600

District 4 Al-Anon Information Service
P.O. Box 19353
Orlando, FL 32814 • (305) 647-3333

AFG Information Service
P.O. Box 1708
Tampa, FL 33601 • (813) 229-8001

Palm Beach Family Groups Information Service
P.O. Box 1229
West Palm Beach, FL 33402
Telephone: (305) 845-4984

GEORGIA
Metro Atlanta Al-Anon/Alateen
Information Service
Suite 107
173 W. Wieuca Rd., N.E.
Atlanta, GA 30342 • (404) 843-0311

District VII and District XX
Information Service Al-Anon
P.O. Box 444
Cobb, GA 31735 • (912) 888-1629

HAWAII
AFG of Hawaii
P.O. Box 730
Waimea, HI 96796

IDAHO
Al-Anon/Alateen Information Service Center
P.O. Box 2524
Boise, ID 83701 • (208) 344-1661

Panhandle Al-Anon Intergroup
2117 Boyd
Coeur D'Alene, ID 83814 • (208) 666-1393

Al-Anon Intergroup Service
P.O. Box 2761
Idaho Falls, ID 83401 • (208) 524-3532

ILLINOIS
Al-Anon/Alateen Information Service
P.O. Box 35
Addison, IL 60101 • (312) 627-4441

Al-Anon/Alateen Information Service
4259 S. Archer Avenue, 2nd Floor
Chicago, IL 60632 • (312) 890-1141

Al-Anon/Alateen Information Service
P.O. Box 183
Crystal Lake, IL 60014 • (815) 459-6190

Al-Anon Information Service Office
P.O. Box 388
Decatur, IL 62525 • (217) 422-3766

Al-Anon-Alateen Information Service
P.O. Box 151
East Moline, IL 61244 • (309) 797-5126

Al-Anon/Alateen Information Service
P.O. Box 3423
Joliet, IL 60434 • (815) 723-9386

District 1A Information Service Al-Anon
P.O. Box 974
Libertyville, IL 60048 • (312) 949-6770

Al-Anon/Alateen Information Service
715 Lake Street, Room 131
Oak Park, IL 60301 • (312) 848-2707

Al-Anon/Alateen Information Service
P.O. Box 94784
Schaumburg, IL 60194 • (312) 358-0338

Al-Anon/Alateen Information Service
P.O. Box 693
Sterling, IL 61081 • (815) 626-8797

S. Cook County Al-Anon/Alateen
Information Service
P.O. Box 1
Worth, IL 60001 • (312) 471-0225

INDIANA

Elkhart Al-Anon Information Intergroup
P.O. Box 1202
Elkhart, IN 46515 • (219) 293-8939

Al-Anon Ft. Wayne Area Intergroup
2212 So. Calhoun Street
Ft. Wayne, IN 46804 • (219) 484-7282

Indianapolis Al-Anon Information Service
5632 E. Washington Street
Indianapolis, IN 46219 • (317) 356-3744

Al-Anon/Alateen Information Service
1511 Liberty, Apt. 1
Mishawaka, IN 46545 • (219) 256-5820

Al-Anon Information Service
345 1/2 Lincolnway West
South Bend, IN 46601 • (219) 288-1650

IOWA

Al-Anon District 9 Information Service
206 Salem
Blue Grass, IA 52726 • (319) 381-1202

Al-Anon Information Service District 7
P.O. Box 425
Des Moines, IA 50302 • (515) 282-1385

Al-Anon Information Center
Insurance Exch. Bldg.
507 7th Street, Room 238
Sioux City, IA 51101 • (712) 255-6724

KANSAS

Al-Anon Information Service
Johnson-Wyandotte Co.
14311 W. 83rd Place
Lenexa, Kansas 66215 • (913) 384-4653

Wichita Information Service
P.O. Box 2308
Wichita, KS 67202 • (316) 266-8499

KENTUCKY

Northern Kentucky Information Service
P.O. Box 17332
Ft. Mitchell, KY 41017 • (606) 491-5071

Al-Anon Information Service
P.O. Box 8184—Station E
Louisville, KY 40208 • (502) 245-1381

LOUISIANA

Al-Anon Information Service
2351 Energy Drive, Suite 1012
Baton Rouge, LA 70808 • (504) 343-0613

Al-Anon/Alateen Information Service
P.O. Box 90041
Lafayette, LA 70509 • (318) 988-2681

Greater New Orleans Al-Anon Intergroup
Independence Mall II, Suite A-8
4241 Veterans Blvd.
Metairie, LA 70002 • (504) 241-9013

Al-Anon Information Service
P.O. Box 385
Shreveport, LA 71162 • (318) 742-3986

MARYLAND

Al-Anon Information Service
P.O. Box 6826
Baltimore, MD 21285 • (301) 823-1222

Mary-Del Tri-Co. Al-Anon
Information Service
P.O. Box 561
North East, MD 21901 • (301) 939-4690

Anne Arundel County Al-Anon
Information Service
P.O. Box 763
Severna Park, MD 21146 • (301) 766-1984

MASSACHUSETTS

Al-Anon Family Groups of Massachusetts Inc.
460 Washington Street, Room 1
Braintree, MA 02184 • (617) 843-5300

Al-Anon/Alateen Information Center
P.O. Box 307
306 Main Street
West Dennis, MA 02670 • (617) 394-4555

MICHIGAN

District 5 Information Service
1475 Westfield
Ann Arbor, MI 48103 • (313) 995-4949

Al-Anon Information Service of Oakland County
25 W. Longlake Rd. #103
Bloomfield Hills, MI 48013 • (313) 647-0021

Al-Anon Family Groups of Detroit Area
13814 E. 7 Mile Road
Detroit, MI 48205 • (313) 527-4610

Genesee Area Al-Anon Information Service
P.O. Box 3493
Flint, MI 48502 • (313) 234-1460

Al-Anon Information Service of Grand Rapids
P.O. Box 1428
Grand Rapids, MI 49501 • (616) 956-6166

MINNESOTA

Al-Anon/Alateen Information Service
Center of District K
3005 Restormel Street
Duluth, MN 55802 • (218) 624-2764

Al-Anon/Alateen Information Service of
Greater Minneapolis
4100 Vernon Avenue S: Room #5
Minneapolis, MN 55416 • (612) 920-3961

Fargo-Moorhead Al-Anon Information Service
P.O. Box 1285
Moorhead, MN 56560 • (701) 293-0291

A.F.G. Information Center
1538 White Bear Ave.
Suite 201
St. Paul, MN 55106 • (612) 771-2208

MISSISSIPPI
Jackson Area Al-Anon Intergroup
555 Hartfield Street
Jackson, MS 39216 • (601) 362-3546

MISSOURI
Al-Anon Information Service
1012 N. Main Suite B
Independence, MO 64050 • (816) 254-1405

Al-Anon Information Center
2683 S. Big Bend Suite 17
St. Louis, MO 63143 • (314) 645-1572

MONTANA
Great Falls Al-Anon Intergroup
P.O. Box 135
Great Falls, MT 59403 • (406) 453-2512

NEBRASKA
Lincoln Al-Anon/Alateen Intergroup
P.O. Box 30082
Lincoln, NE 68503 • (402) 477-9662

Al-Anon Information Service Inc.
3929 Harney Street
Rm 230
Omaha, NE 68131 • (402) 345-2414

NEVADA
Southern Nevada Al-Anon Information Service
P.O. Box 43271
Las Vegas, NV 89104 • (702) 642-7438

Northern Nevada Al-Anon Information Service
P.O. Box 10093, Main Station
Reno, NV 89510 • (702) 348-7103

NEW JERSEY
South Jersey Information Service
116 White Horse Pike Ave. 1B.
Haddon Heights, NJ 08035 • (609) 428-0083

Al-Anon/Alateen Information Service of North Jersey
73 South Fullerton Ave. Room 303
Montclair, NJ 07042 • (201) 744-8686

NEW MEXICO
Al-Anon Information Service
1923 Alvarado NE #9
Albuquerque, NM 87110 • (505) 262-2177

Al-Anon Information Service
P.O. Box 2285
Hobbs, NM 88241 • (505) 393-8542 or 393-5432

NEW YORK
Al-Anon Help Line
P.O. Box 591
Chappaqua, NY 10514 • (914) 241-8444

AFG Information Service of Western N.Y.
P.O. Box 37
Cheektowaga, NY 14225 • (716) 856-2520

Suffolk Al-Anon Information Service
Box H
Farmingville, NY 11738 • (516) 654-2827

Greater New York Al-Anon Family Intergroup
200 Park Ave. S. Room 1602
New York, NY 10003 • (212) 254-7230

Al-Anon Information Service
74 Lake Ave.
Rochester, NY 14608 • (716) 442-2290

Al-Anon Information Service
423 W. Onondaga St.
Syracuse, NY 13202 • (315) 471-0191

Nassau Al-Anon Information Service
P.O. Box 755
Westbury, NY 11590 • (516) 222-0556

NORTH CAROLINA
Al-Anon Information Service
P.O. Box 35321
Charlotte, NC 28235 • (704) 333-9523

Al-Anon Information Service
P.O. Box 217
Greensboro, NC 27402 • (919) 272-4493

Al-Anon/Alateen Service Office
P.O. Box 18731
Raleigh, NC 27619-8731 • (919) 787-1653

Wilmington Al-Anon Information Service
P.O. Box 5363
Wilmington, NC 28403 • (919) 762-6637

OHIO
Akron Area Al-Anon Intergroup
P.O. Box 1071
Akron, OH 44309 • (216) 253-4000

Greater Cincinnati Information Service
P.O. Box 665
Cincinnati, OH 45202 • (513) 891-2055

Al-Anon Information Service
One Public Square Bldg.
Suite 712
Cleveland, OH 44113 • (216) 621-1381

Al-Anon Information Service Dist. 1
1706 E. Broad St.
Columbus, OH 43203 • (614) 253-2701

Miami Valley Information Service
P.O. Box 282
Dayton, OH 45401 • (513) 274-7871

Golden Crescent Information Service
P.O. Box 664
Lorain, OH 44052 • (216) 277-6969

Al-Anon Information Service
2151 Rush Boulevard
Youngstown, OH 44507 • (216) 533-3361

OKLAHOMA
Al-Anon Information Service
2720 N. Classen, #103
Oklahoma City, OK 73106 • (405) 528-5290

Tulsa A.F.G. Intergroup Service Office
2326 South Garnett, Suite 1
Tulsa, OK 74129 • (918) 371-7287

OREGON
Al-Anon Information Service
P.O. Box 2413
Eugene, OR 97402 • (503) 741-2841

Al-Anon Information Service
1750 S.W. Skyline Blvd., Box 4
Portland, OR 97221 • (503) 292-1333

Salem Al-Anon Information Service
P.O. Box 717
Salem, OR 97308 • (503) 370-7363

PENNSYLVANIA
Altoona Helping Hands Al-Anon Intergroup
P.O. Box 429
Altoona, PA 16603 • (814) 946-9002

Al-Anon Intergroup Service of Delaware Valley
4021 Walnut St.
Philadelphia, PA 19104 • (215) 222-5244

Al-Anon Information Service
P.O. Box 3693
Pittsburgh, PA 15230 • (412) 321-1882

Al-Anon Intergroup
State College—Area
426 Shadow Lane
State College, PA 16801

District 7 Al-Anon Information Service
P.O. Box 47
West Chester, PA 19381 • (215) 696-4216

PUERTO RICO
Al-Anon Information
P. O. Box 3979
Bayamon Garden Station
Bayamon, PR 00620 • (809) 787-2635

RHODE ISLAND
Rhode Island Al-Anon Information Center
769 Park Avenue
Cranston, RI 02910 • (401) 785-9722

SOUTH CAROLINA
Greenville Al-Anon Intergroup
c/o Alano Club
111 Catlina Dr.
Greenville, SC 29609 • (803) 277-5606

Spartanburg Al-Anon Intergroup
103 Castleford Road
Moore, SC 29369 • (803) 574-4514

SOUTH DAKOTA
Al-Anon Service Center—District 2
402 Quincy Street
Rapid City, SD 57701 • (605) 348-9113

TENNESSEE
Dist. 12 Al-Anon/Alateen Public Information Service
Route 2, Box 334 Cherry Road
Goodlettsville, TN 37072 • (615) 385-3262

Al-Anon Information Service
1913 Clematis Dr.
Hixson, TN 37343 • (615) 842-1034

Knox Area District Al-Anon Information Service
P.O. Box 1467
Knoxville, TN 37901 • (615) 522-7535

Al-Anon Information Service
2962 Meadow Brook Dr.
Memphis, TN 38109 • (901) 766-9733

TEXAS
Al-Anon Information Service
P.O. Box 2524
Amarillo, TX 79105 • (806) 373-2297

Al-Anon Information Center
5526 Dyer, Suite 208
Dallas, TX 75206 • (214) 363-0461

Al-Anon Information Service
P.O. Box 26285
El Paso, TX 79926 • (915) 532-2173

Al-Anon/Alateen Information Service
1203 Lake, Suite 207
Fort Worth, TX 76102 • (817) 336-2492

Al-Anon Family Group Service
3202 Wesleyan, Suite 220
Houston, TX 77027 • (713) 965-9026

Al-Anon Information Service
P.O. Box 10677
Lubbock, TX 79408 • (806) 796-8001

Al-Anon Information Service
908 Boston Avenue
Nederland, TX 77627 • (409) 721-9391

Group 12 AFG Office
Club 12
102 Thames
San Antonio, TX 78216 • (512) 433-3584

UTAH
Utah Area Al-Anon/Alateen
Info. Service Center
5056 South 300 West
Murray, UT 84107 • (801) 262-9587

Al-Anon Information Center
Ballon Place Room 346
2433 Adams Street
Ogden, UT 84401 • (801) 621-1654

VIRGINIA
Al-Anon Service Center of Northern Virginia
200 Park Avenue Room 300
Falls Church, VA 22046 • (703) 241-2011

Al-Anon Information Service of Tidewater
Penbroke One, Suite 400
281 Independence Blvd.
Virginia Beach, VA 23462 • (804) 499-1443

WASHINGTON
Al-Anon Information Service
1402 3rd Ave.
Vance Bldg. #921
Seattle, WA 98101 • (206) 625-0000

Pierce County Al-Anon Information Service
P.O. Box 11395
Tacoma, WA 98411 • (206) 272-3081

Al-Anon Information Service
P.O. Box 2597
Vancouver, WA 98668 • (206) 695-1496

WISCONSIN
Al-Anon Family Groups of S.E. Wisconsin
8320 West Bluemound Rd. Room 209
Milwaukee, WI 53213 • (414) 257-2415

WYOMING
Round Table Intergroup
P.O. Box 9805
Casper, WY 82609 • (307) 234-5160

Cheyenne AFG Intergroup
P.O. Box 2823
Cheyenne, WY 82003-2823
Telephone: (307) 632-6764

CANADA

Al-Anon Family Groups Canada
National Public Information Committee
P.O. Box 6433
Station J
Ottawa, Canada K2A 3Y6
Telephone: (613) 722-1830

ALBERTA
Al-Anon Central Service Office
#414-815 1st Street, SW,
Calgary, Alberta, Canada T2P 1N3
Telephone: (403) 266-6215

BRITISH COLUMBIA
Al-Anon/Alateen Information Service
P.O. Box 2174
Dawson Creek, B.C., Canada V1G 4K9
Telephone: (604) 782-4663

Al-Anon Information Center
Box 14
Kamloops, B.C., Canada V2B 6S4
Telephone: (604) 372-8046

Al-Anon Central Services
P.O. Box 2333
Vancouver, B.C., Canada V6B 3W5
Telephone: (604) 688-1716

Al-Anon Information Service
P.O. Box 654
Victoria, B.C., Canada V8W 2P3
Telephone: (604) 682-0744

MANITOBA
Al-Anon Central Services of Manitoba
304-310 Donald St.
Winnipeg, Manitoba, Canada R3B 2H4
Telephone: (204) 943-6051

NOVA SCOTIA
Al-Anon Information Service
53 Portland Street, Suite 4
Nova Scotia, Canada B2Y 1H1
Telephone: (902) 466-7077

ONTARIO
Al-Anon Central Office
2453 Yonge St., Suite 7
Toronto, Ontario, Canada M4P 2E8
Telephone: (416) 486-1888

Al-Anon Information Service
P.O. Box 4331
London, Ontario, Canada N5W 5J6
Telephone: (519) 672-7310

Al-Anon Information Service
P.O. Box 161, Station "S"
Toronto, Ontario, Canada M5M 4L7
Telephone: (416) 366-4072

District No. Seven Information Service
Box 181
Vermilion Bay, Ontario, Canada P0V 2V0
Telephone: (807) 227-2758

QUEBEC—ENGLISH
Al-Anon Information Service (English)
Dewittville Post Office
Dewittville, Quebec, Canada J0S 1C0
Telephone: (514) 264-4481

QUEBEC—FRENCH
Publications Francaises P.F.A. Inc.
P.O. Box 266
Montreal, Quebec, Canada H2V 4N1
Telephone: (514) 389-5043

Service D'Information Al-Anon
P.O. Box 114, Station "C"
Montreal, Quebec, Canada H2L 4J7
Telephone: (514) 729-3034

SASKATCHEWAN
Al-Anon/Alateen Information Service
#11-2425 13th Avenue
Regina, Saskatchewan
Canada S4P 0W1
Telephone: (306) 522-7500

Al-Anon Intergroup
P.O. Box 1184
100 5 Ave. N.
Saskatoon, Saskatchewan
Canada S7K 3M2
Telephone: (306) 665-8434

UNITED KINGDOM

ENGLAND
*Al-Anon Family Groups U.K. & Eire
61 Great Dover Street
London, England SE1 4YF
Telephone: 01-403-0888

NORTHERN IRELAND
Belfast Al-Anon Information Service
RM. 8, Cathedral Bldgs.
64 Donegal Street
Belfast, Antrim
Northern Ireland
Telephone: 243-489

SCOTLAND
Al-Anon Information Service
136 Ingram St.
Glasgow G11 EJ, Scotland
Telephone: 041-552-2828

REPUBLIC OF IRELAND

Al-Anon Information Service
12 Westmoreland Street
Dublin 2, Ireland
Telephone: 01-774-195

Supplied by Al-Anon Family Group Headquarters, Inc.

You can call the Alcohol Helpline for additional phone numbers and further information. (see page 81)

Further Reading

Perhaps your librarian will order a book, or obtain it from inter-library loan, if you are not successful in finding one of these books in your local library.

FOR VERY YOUNG CHILDREN

Black, Claudia. *My Dad Loves Me, My Dad Has a Disease.* ACT, P.O. Box 8536, Newport Beach, CA 92660.

NONFICTION FOR MOST READERS

Babor, Thomas. *Alcohol: Customs and Rituals.* New York: Chelsea House, 1986.

Brooks, Cathleen. *The Secret Everyone Knows.* San Diego, Calif: Operation Cork, 1981.

Claypool, Jane. *Alcohol and Teens.* New York: Messner, 1985.

Cohen, Susan and Daniel. *A Six-pack and a Fake I.D.: Teens Look at the Drinking Question.* New York: M. Evans and Company, 1986.

Girouard, Mark. *Victorian Pubs.* New Haven, Conn.: Yale University Press, 1984.

Hornick, Edith. *You and Your Alcoholic Parent.* New York: Associated Press, 1974.

Lang, Alan R., *Alcohol: Teenage Drinking.* New York: Chelsea House, 1985.

Ryerson, Eric. *When Your Parent Drinks Too Much: A Book for Teenagers.* New York: Facts on File, 1985.

Seixas, Judith S. *Living With A Parent That Drinks Too Much.* New York: Greenwillow Books, 1979.

Seixas, J.S. and Youcha, G. *Children of Alcoholism: A Survivor's Manual.* New York: Crown Publishers, 1985.

Wagner, Robin S. *Sarah T: Portrait of a Teen-age Alcoholic.* New York: Ballantine Books, 1975.

FICTION FOR MOST READERS

Donovan, John. *I'll Get There. It Better Be Worth the Trip.* New York: Harper, 1969.

Dorman, N. B. *Laughter in the Background.* New York: Lodestar, 1980.

Holland, Isabelle. *Heads You Win, Tails I Lose.* Philadelphia: Lippincott, 1973.

Kerr, M.E. *The Son of Someone Famous.* New York: Harper, 1974.

Neville, Emily Cheney. *Garden of Broken Glass.* New York: Delacorte, 1975.

Oppenheimer, Joan. *Francesca, Baby.* New York: Scholastic, 1976.

Seabrook, Brenda. *Home Is Where They Take You In.* New York: Morrow, 1980.

Stolz, Mary. *The Edge of Next Year.* New York: Harper, 1974.

———. *What Time of Night Is It?* New York: Holiday, 1979.

Wolkoff, Judie. *Where the Elf King Sings.* Scarsdale, N.Y.: Bradbury, 1980.

Zindel, Paul. *Pardon Me, You're Stepping on My Eyeball.* New York: Harper, 1976.

Glossary

absorption—The process by which alcohol goes from the stomach and small intestines into the bloodstream.

abstainer—A person who does not drink alcohol. Many people dislike having their minds and bodies influenced by this drug.

alcoholism—A disease that progresses to uncontrolled drinking. It is characterized by physical dependence on alcohol.

Alcoholics Anonymous (AA)—A worldwide organization of recovering alcoholics. Members meet to discuss their problems related to alcohol so they can continue to avoid drinking and help others with their drinking problems.

Al-Anon—A worldwide organization of wives and husbands of alcoholics. Members meet to discuss their problems. A list of groups can be found on pages 82-88.

Alateen—An organization for teenagers who have a parent or parents who are alcoholics. Members meet to discuss their problems with their parent(s) and to learn how to enjoy their own lives. A list of local groups can be found on page 82-88.

bender—A long period of drunkenness, such as two or three days.

blackout—Being unable to remember what one said or did and what happened when one was drunk.

distillation—Heating wine or beer to turn the alcohol into a gas. This gas is then cooled and becomes liquid alcohol, or distilled spirits.

drug—Anything that people put on their skin or swallow that can have an effect on how their minds or bodies work. Examples of drugs include caffeine (in tea, coffee, cocoa), nicotine (in cigarettes), aspirin, penicillin, PCP, heroin, and alcohol.

drunk—The way people feel and act when they have drunk enough alcohol to cause them to lose most or all control of their actions and thoughts. Same as intoxicated.

drunk and disorderly—Actions of a person who is drunk and acting out (yelling, screaming, disturbing the peace). This is a crime in many states.

D.T.'s (delirium tremens)—Trembling, nausea, hallucinations, and insomnia caused by sudden withdrawal of alcohol from an addicted body.

ethyl alcohol—The *only* kind of alcohol that is safe to drink. It is made from fruits and cereals.

fermentation—Yeast acting on the sugar in fruit juices or cereals to produce alcohol, which can be used to make wine or beer.

hangover—The sick feeling most people feel several hours after having been drunk or high. Hangovers happen after the alcohol has left the body and the drinker is sober.

legal drinking age—The age at which a person can legally buy alcohol in liquor stores, restaurants, and bars.

methyl alcohol—A type of alcohol that is poisonous if drunk. It is made from wood and is sometimes called wood alcohol. It is found in antifreeze, paint thinners, fuels, and so on.

oxidation—The process in which the liver adds oxygen to alcohol in the body to produce carbon dioxide, water, and energy.

peer—A person who is your age and has the same social position. "Peer pressure" happens when people with no special authority or power try to get other people like them to do, or not to do, something.

problem drinker—A person whose drinking causes problems for him or her or for other people.

proof—The word used to describe the amount of alcohol in distilled spirits. One degree of proof equals 0.5 percent alcohol.

sedative—A drug that calms people. Alcohol can act as a sedative.

skid row—A part of town where homeless people live. Many "skid-row bums" are not problem drinkers.

sober—Not high or drunk. In control of what one says or does.

social drinker—A person who drinks alcohol but does not drink enough to cause any problem.

This glossary is based on information supplied by the United States Department of Health and Human Services.

Index

A

abstinence, 9
Adult Children of Alcoholics, 49
Al-Anon, *40*, 52, 55, 58, 59, 81,
    82-88
Alateen, *40*, 45, 51, 52, 53, 54
alcohol
    as acne medicine, 25
    as an addictive drug, 7
    an anti-infection medicine, 25
    in the body, 26-35
    as cause of death and injury, 18, 19
    and effect on brain, 30, 32, *33*, 34
    as fuel, 25
    use in magic and medicine, 13
    in nature, 12
    and pregnancy, 31
    and sex, 32
    as stress relief, 29
alcoholic content, 20, 24
alcoholic parents, 38, 39, 49-54, 74
Alcoholics Anonymous, 39, 41, 52, 55
alcoholics, percentage of population, 7
alcoholism
    biological factors, 9, 37, 74
    as cause of family problems, 16,
      49-56
    causes of, 37-39
    as a disease, 9, 10, 13, 19, 41, 46,
      51, 53, 58, 74
    environmental factors, 9, 37, 74
    extent of, 16
    kinds of, 37, 74
    genetic factors, 9, 37-39, 74
    as learned behavior, 9
    as a public health problem, 18
American beers, 21
attitudes about drinking, 19, 58

B

B vitamins, 46
beer, 10, 15, 21, 23, 28, 43, 44, 45,
    51, 66, 75
Begleiter, Henri, 38
Belize, 71
birth defects, 30, 76
blackouts, 46, 55, 74

blood, 26, 27, 36
bourbon, 13, 21
brain wave patterns, 38
brandy, 22
breast cancer, 29

C

calories, 21, 28, 48, 73
carbon dioxide, 21
caveman, 12
children of alcoholics, 37-39, 49-56,
    74
Children of Alcoholics Foundation
    (COAF), 81
cholesterol, 29
cider, 71
cirrhosis, 27
cognac, 22
congeners, 21
cordials, 22
cortisol, 38
crack, 74

D

D.T.'s (delirium tremens), 45
dieting, 28
digestive system, 24
distilled spirits, 13, 14, 16, 21, 22
drinking age, 7, 23, 74, 79
drunk driving, 7, 18, 64-65, 75
drunkenness, 7, 14, 18, 27, 28

E

early alcoholism, 40-41, 48, 55
empty calories, 28-29, 74
Eskimos, 74
ethyl alcohol, 25
experimental drug, 28

F

family therapy, 18
"fatty liver," 27
fermentation process, 20-21
fetal alcohol syndrome, 30-*31*
Finland study of twins, 38
fortified wines, 20

S

Scotch, 21
self-test, 40-41
sexual relations, 32
Shakespeare, 32
sherry, 20
Shuckit, Marc, 38, 39
skid-row bum, 6
social drinking, 9, 10-11, 48, 75, 77
State University of New York Health
    Center, 38
STOPP-A-TEER, 68-69
stout, 21
Students Against Driving Drunk
    (SADD), 65, 80
SADD Contract for Life, 65, 80
Students to Offset Peer Pressure
    (STOPP), 67-71
sugar, 11, 20-21

T

TARGET, 71
temperance tract, 15
testosterone, 32
twins, 38

U

United Way, 65
University of California at San Diego,
    38
University of Kansas, 38

V

Virginia Colony Drunkenness Law, 15-
    16
vitamins, 46
vodka, 13, 21

W

whiskey, 21, *22*
wine, 7, 10, *11*, 13, 14, *17*, 20, 21,
    23, 24, 75
wine coolers, 21, 22
wine making, 20
World Kid's Congress, 69

Y

yeast, 12, 20-21
young alcoholics and abusers, 18, 39,
    42-48